MW01469427

Jimmy Jazz **III** Complete Works

1 House of the Unwed Mother

2 The Cadillac Tramps

3 The Sub

4 M-Theory

5 Rube Goldberg Suicide Machine

6 Where Life is Inappropriate

7 Home Despot

8 Nothing a Fire Can't Fix

9 This Ragged Muscle

10 The Book of Books

NOTHING A FIRE CAN'T FIX

POEMS BY JIMMY JAZZ

[signature] 2022

Pirate Enclave BOOKS

21/50

©2022 by Jimmy Jazz

First Edition

ISBN: 978-1-73-586860-8

Book Design: Jimmy Jazz

FRANCHISE, **Racing Sans One**, & Avenir were used in the design of this book.

Poems in this volume appeared in chapbooks: Fat Free Lard, Cosmology & Gravitational Collapse, Drapetomania, Pollycide, & Boom Schlim Ba-LA-LA Loon.

Pirate Enclave Books

https://pirateenclave.square.site

NOTHING A FIRE CAN'T FIX ⊗ POEMS

The more you drive, the less intelligent you are.

Miller

I've got bombs in my pockets
    enough anger to launch rockets
        & a heart full of woe

Angela Boyce

Table of Contents

Apes	1
Mantra for a Horny Brain	2
Invocation to a Riot	3
A Car Alarm	5
The Plan	7
Anarchist Think Tank	8
Humpity Dumpity	9
Sleep, Sex, Eat, & Drink	9
Big Bang Theory	10
El Poemo Negro	11
The Nostalgia Hounds	16
I'm Not an Artist	17
Empty Metaphors	17
Smash the Vacuum to Free the Filament	18
Passionate Performers	19
After Willam	20
A Jimmy Jazz Poem	21
Bees	22
ANGELA	23
Grammar	24
After Emily	24
Dumpster	24
Traps	24
Jonas Salk	25
A Fire	25
Shall I compare Thee Sunday Drive?	26
The Fleas I've Killed	27
Espresso ex machina	27
Amputation	27
Spy	28
La Posta	28
Untitled	28
Pinball Fixation	29
Belief	30
The Impossibility of an Anti-banana Poem	31
Desiré Said	32
Pick Up Milk on a Beer Run?	32
A Good Heart	33
Ashtray	33
Nostalgic Rock	34
Walking Past the Church	36
Mmmmmmmm	36
Presidents	36
Urban Legend	37
When The Neighbor Gets Shot	38

We Are Here	39
Humanity	40
Johnny Thunders Was Murdered	41
Unrequited Love	42
Elegy for Jim	43
Poem to a Mormon Father	46
Vodka Tonic	47
Bottle O Wine	47
I'm Not a Scientist	48
Perturbative Approach	48
Quantum Mechanic	48
The Red Jeans	49
The Free Way	51
Denial	51
Conservation	51
In the Studio	52
Granny	53
Chiapas 45	54
The Johnson Family	56
Stuckism	58
Newton's Sleep	60
Beauty = Symmetry	60
Drunk Blues	61
Piaf	63
An Idea	63
Identity Zero	64
Tell the Revolutionary Court to Hang the Meterpigs First	65
Our Inside-out Love Story	69
A Student	70
Fishing	70
The Cat Leaps	70
Old Head	71
Social Einsteinism	72
Balzac's 60 Cups	73
Touching Madness	74
Martin Luther King Parade	75
X & Y	76
Pain is Pain	77
Small Pox	78
Walking Fuck Machine	80
Anthropic Principle	81
Saint Tersea	82
Bad Religion	83
Jesse's Mom Beats Him	84
Bile	85
Blades of Grass	88

Pessimist	88
Diet	88
I Cannot Leave This Human World	89
The Rhythm of Inertia	90
Electroweak Theory	91
The Ruse Eviction	92
Stupid Daydreams	94
Writers Livers	96
A Wedding	96
After a week without coffee, I dreamt of wild horses	97
Allen Ginsberg	99
Roman Midwinter Festival Tree	100
The Sun Called	100
Slingshot	104
The Observable Universe	104
My Aunt, My Mother's Sister	105
Saturday Morning Whittles Away	109
Weirdo	109
Film Students	110
Cecil	110
Paradigm Shift	110
I Wanna Be Your Roach	111
History in the Document Shredder	112
Is 74 old Enough?	114
The Untried States of Poetry	115
Minimalist Museum	116
Event Horizon	131
Black Hole	131
Strange Attractor	131
Memory Palace	132
How Refreshing	134
A Little Brainless Child	136
Oblivion	136
Life Savers	136
Educational Experience	137
Employee of the Month	138
I Am a Moron	139
Coffee Shop Hip Hop	140
They Say	141
The Pig Ritual	142
The Philatelist	145
Threadbare	145
Poverty	145
Consensual Sex Among The Turtles	146
Turtle	146
Anthropotactique	147

Einstein-Rosen Bridge	148
Racist Bomb Threat	149
Killing Time	150
Free Lunch	151
Jack Hirschman, Jack Marshall, Jack Spicer	151
Stolen Car	152
The Club	153
Bruises of Mood (black Blues)	155
Iterations	156
Short Lines	157
Riemannian Geometry	158
Schrödinger's Cat	158
Where Life is Inappropriate	159
Running for Chomsky	160
Watched the Life & Times of Allen Ginsberg	162
You are Your Right Hand	164
Doremequisha	165
1937	166
A Lovely Evening of Useless Erudition	168
False Vacuum	169
Gum Control	170
Discouragement	171
Portents	172
Easy to Understand	173
Tenderness	174
Spreadsheets	175
Humans Use Tools	176
Polar Eyes	178
The Einstein-Bohr Debate	182
More Sorrentinos	183
mud pie & the titty	186
Fruit Fly	186
Long Day	186
I Have Ugly Gray Dog Balls	187
The Cure	188
Beach Towel	188
Book Fair	188
Free Thinking	189
Grumbling	189
Nervous Breakdown	190
The Cosmological Constant	191
Karma	192
Tired Mind	193
Now I Am The Cancer	194
Quitting Stuff	195
My Daydream	198

Common Senses	199
The Humiliation of Work	202
General Relativity	204
Heisenberg's Uncertainty Principle	204
The Coupling Constant	204
Meditations	205
Wine Stains	206
Strummer	207
My Uncle, My Mother's Brother	210
A Skirmish	212
Gila Bend	213
String Theory	214
A Poem for Janice Jordan	215
Dragging My Ass Through the Day	217
Anxious Beats	219
THE CUBE	220
The Tyranny of Pants	221
Schadenfreude	223
Graveyard Shift	224
Singularity	226
Death's Cousin	227
¡Voila!	228
FOIA Request	229
The Silence	231
Small Talk	232
The Kiss	233
A Reef	240
When Physicists Talk About God	241
Train Whistles	242
Obligations	242
Doing Just One Thing	243
Helper	244
Slumming For Kidneys	246
Falling Asleep in Front of the TV	247
Go Sleep Off the Booze Night	248
Race Based Admissions	249
Decoherence	250
The Reality	251
Humming	252
The Après Garde	253
Rushmore	255
Certainty	255
TWAT	255
The Last Piece of Shit	256

INTRODUCTION

Blake, Wordsworth, Coleridge, Keats, Shelley, Bukowski, Jim Carroll, Patti Smith, Exene Cervenka, Lydia Lunch, Henry Miller, Kerouac, Ginsberg, Burroughs, Karen Finley, The Last Poets, Tamara Johnson, Kevin Chanel, Shinya, Patrick Haley, Chris Galante, Nicole, Pas, Jesusita, Gary Hustwit, Pleasant Gehman, Iris Berry, Nicole Panter, Liz Belie, Steve Abee, Barry Graham, Peter Plate, Jervey Tervalon, Cole Heinowitz, Dave Alvin, Richard Loranger, Crisa, Juliette Torrez, Mud Baron, Shappy, Maggie Estep, Michelle Serros, Wammo, Matt Cook, The Casbah, Noelle b, MI Blue, Jahson Edmonds, Goldfish, Angela Boyce, The Free*stars, Several Girls Galore, Creedle, Stewart Home, Hal Sirowitz, Shawna Kenney, Daphne Gottlieb, Jeffrey McDaniel, Jennifer Jospeh, Ellyn Maybe, Regie Cabico, Douglas A. Martin, Justin Chin, June Melby, Shawn Kenney, Dennis Cooper, reg e. gaines, Tarin Towers, Beth Lisick, Bucky Sinister, Jennifer Joseph, Jon Longhi, Larry Fondation, Rich Ferguson, Alexis O'Hara, Matthew Niblock, Jubilee Dunbar, Linda Albertano, LA Ruocco, Clebo Rainey, Victor Infante, Jack Evans, Lob, The Watts Prophets, Sandra Zane, Stickman X, Quincy Troupe, Sandra Alcosser, Cry of the Eagle, Craig Foltz, Sev Reyes, Rae Armantrout, Adrian Arancibia, Miguel-Angel Soria, Jerome Rothenberg, Mary Williams, minerva, Lizzie Wann, Chris Vannoy, Derrick Brown, Hank Hyena, Upski, Mary Leary, Gary Glazner, Saul Williams, Brett Axel, Michael Hemmingson, Ted Washington, Pat Payne, Kimberly Dark, Michael Klam, Robert O'Sullivan, Vejea Jennings, Don Bajema, Cecil Hayduke, Poetry the Klown.

Jimmy Jazz 2022

APES

The poetry of existential angst
begins in a shower
sitting
naked knees to chest
water on skin, rain masking rivulets
when The Other comes
knowing
stripping to kneel
or joining dressed
at once distinguishing salt
with lips pressed
slipping into the nape to shake the jugular
we sometimes clench fists at the heavens
alternating lines:

        What
        does
        it
        all
        mean?

with each our pain rubbing like sticks
to make fire against the cold
which moves toward us like a wave in a fog
holding on until steam dissipates
one pulling the other
to stand & start again

MANTRA FOR A HORNY BRAIN

My Brain is horny, my body is not
My Brain is horny, my body is not
My Brain is horny, my body is not
My Brain is horny, my body is not
My Brain is horny, my body is not

INVOCATION TO A RIOT

Little locked in your room poem writing mother fuckers waiting for permission from the muse to go wild, go crazy!

How long you gonna wait for inspiration to send your inhibitions on vacation?

How long you gonna be a shit-eating dreamer slaving for the man?

How long you gonna work a job you hate?

Never thought I'd hate my job
Never thought I'd kill myself
Never thought I'd fall in love with you-hoo-hoo

So it's a pop song this life of ours?
Or a poetry reading?

This is not a poetry reading
(Ceci n'est pas une lecture de poesie)

I am the Incredulous Hulk of spoken word

Listen to your brothers' call
BREAK DOWN
The prison walls…

I'm banging my head on the world
I'm banging my head on the world

Live dangerously
Think about masturbation
Go down on your knees often to meditate or copulate
Pride is delusion
Art is an answer
Money isn't even a good band-aid
Work is stupid, it makes you tired

Nothing a Fire Can't Fix

Entropy takes care of itself

If a stranger asks to give you a blow job, say yes

Angela Boyce said, *I am art.*

Tamara Johnson said, *Am I dead or am I alive?*
And if I'm dead, who will tell me?

And Michael Klam said, The early bird is the first to get shot.

We can conquer the world by refusing to conquer the world

We can care for aging elders, live with other races,
make equal the sexes, tax the 1%

We can seek pleasure without guilt
We can be the gadfly in the tyrant's face

We can stop the war
…
We can
We can

> *worship the mole on the belly of an exquisite whore*
> *spoil the child & spare the rod*

It's impossible to sell yourself to god

Announcer: Tonight only… Jimmy Jazz

A CAR ALARM

relentless pulsing
somebody steal that fucking car already
i yell inside my head
to drown the incessant noise
which fails to move me to the window
to catch a thief
i could not care less
only resent the intrusion
into my home, the disruption of reading &
some thought

HONK HONK HONK HONK

will it stop? a hell on earth
maybe we're already dead

the most ignominious demise remains
heart failure in a parking garage

II
a car alarm
pulsing & echoing
beneath the foothill sunrise in the east
these past minutes finally stops
the silence
feels like a divot shoveled from the loam of my head…
the silence feels like a hole
the infinite unknown crush of gravity
a hole chewed by a desert-winged moth in my favorite sweater
a rip at the knee of my school pants after mother told me
a hole in the dirt
big enough to bury a hamster
but empty
at this point &
silent

Nothing a Fire Can't Fix

If you kneel & cup your ear,
the faint echo of that stupid car alarm
forever burned into your cells
can still be heard

another phony emergency in the cry-wolf plot
to numb you motionless
against the real & growing pangs of despair
that are the sea of the world

le bateau ivre drifts away

 Boat-less on this island
shovel in hand

THE PLAN

Start with foot-dragging
Sew secret klown suits, bury for use
Stockpile banana peels
Set world record for blowjobs received
Assassinate time
Investigate the correlation between metaphor & caress
Photograph surveillance cameras
Compile dossiers on blissful idiots
Recruit blind surgeons to remove tumors by Braille
Consummate the hate you feel for parents, children, lovers
Become a closet organizer for a wooden shoe collection
Demand reparations from a culture that left you bankrupt

ANARCHIST THINK TANK

When I put out the call to assemble an anarchist think tank, The Queen of Campus Avenue showed up with exotic fish & colored rocks to line the bottom.

My lawyer brought the bail money.

My wife suggested we fill it with hydrogen so the waste would be water.

My daughter brought balls to activate the dunking mechanism.

The shopping cart spinster said to top it with one of those pressure cooker lids her mother used to stew marmalade.

The bearded poet came empty-handed, having set the lobsters free.

Awkward in the shadow of their creative gestures—I hid the turret & heavy treads behind my back.

HUMPITY DUMPITY

I am
hot humpity
horny
to jack off
be nimble
be quick
left hand
one dick

SLEEP, SEX, EAT, & DRINK

I want to eat curry from India & Thailand & even England with chips to dunk & one of those scrumptious Faque Burgers the Seventh Day Adventists sell over on College Avenue & grape leaves stuffed with rice & food give me hummus & tabouli & falafel & those pink pickled turnips & avocado roll & a bean burrito with guacamole & for dessert—yam crusted with brown sugar or mango with sticky rice & two single espressos…

Then this guy tells me,

The path to spirituality starts with denying the body

Nothing a Fire Can't Fix

BIG BANG THEORY

Who compelled the grand succession of presidents to bomb the poorest people in the world?

The Rosicrucians? The Mickey Mouse? Oppenheimer?

Squeaky & Hinkley were insane.

The shot heard round the world was the big bang of American Empire or was that Hiroshima?

Czolgosz didn't help.

        Who said Manifest Destiny ended with Hawaii?

Pax Romana Pax Britannica Pax Americana
What happened to the Ottoman Empire?
Byzantine, Mongol, Qing, Han, Song?

Scientists used to think the universe would expand until it contracted, but it looks like it'll yawn into the void...

Empires expand until they collapse:

This is the law of the jungle, the code of Hammurabi,
the code of the schoolyard.

> *I shall not cause harm to any vehicle nor the personal contents thereof, nor through inaction let that vehicle or the personal contents thereof come to harm.*

Property is Violence / the destruction of property is not peace. Peace will come, later.

The universe expands; empires collapse.
                                      We help.
Cecil's law: When in Rome, do as the Vandals

EL POEMO NEGRO

I
I looked down at my shadow & thought
I was Thelonious Monk
surmising that if a piano materialized on this rooftop
I could play it
by virtue of a goatee & sunglasses

Then I remembered cool doesn't cut it

Downtown Downtown

I lost a blues
by singing instead of writing
I had the groove, but memory has subsided

Alcohol blues
drunk driving & singing blues
We (me & the blues)
were a loud Tom Waits blue
moaning // grunting // ranting
dying inside
in a middle-class white-boy kinda way

A happy death
with soft suffering

II
In the 1970s, we forgot
We forgot what Nazis were
We forgot that the Confederates were slave-owning Nazis

Punks wore swastikas

I thought that orange Charger in The Dukes of Hazzard painted
with the stars & bars was pretty cool

Nothing a Fire Can't Fix

I changed my mind

Patti Smith wrote a song using the word *nigger* which has one meaning when used by black people & another used by white

Patti Smith is white
I am white

She borrowed it from Norman Mailer
who was white

I think she was trying to say Artists like Jimi Hendrix choose to live outside society

outside

the corrupt social order of our majority:
    our sick old men looking for snuff films
    our kiddie porn distribution network
    our Xtian fellowship

But the Confederate good ole boys & all their inbred klan used the word to keep black people out of their society

In a racist culture, you resist or are racist

You can read Malcolm X, listen to hip hop, march for civil rights, Man, you could read all of Toni Morrison twice, but you can't know what it's like to be a black in Amerikkka

Unless you are

III
He wants to be black
He wants to be black
because now it's cool

to be black

Next week he'll be toting
a dashiki to school & back

Just to be black

He likes black music, &
he thinks if he was black,
music would pour from his poor pores

He'd hit on Billie Holiday, if he was black
Hang out with Panthers & fuck shit up

Wouldn't never been no slave
Slit the master's throat & help others do the same—while his black
body was swinging from a tree—

The bulging eyes
The twisted mouth

If he was black, he could make extemporaneous speeches
on the way to martyrdom like Malcolm & Martin

If he was black, women would succumb to his member, which
would be so big as to need its own membership card at Costco

I be going through 600 condoms a week, if I was black

He wants to be black
He wants to jump back
in the alley with brother Little Richard & Long Tall Sally
He wants to be black
 to get back
to a more natural slack
closer to the earth mother
whose breasts are the rivers &
whose feet are the rich dark roots of trees

Nothing a Fire Can't Fix

He wants to be black
to live in the ghetto with a Cadillac
to get back
  Jack
  to shoot smack
    to pimp slap
      He wants to be black

IV
Am I the white devil you're afraid of?
Am I the man been keeping colored folks down?
Have I kept your children from reading?
Do I run this crazy town?

I saw the white devil hiding in the skyline
  —Check the tall building on the right

I saw the white devil lurking behind the bank window
  —He was looking out or was that me looking in?

I saw the white devil's face on the almighty dollar
  —His hand was in my pocket trying to jerk me around

I saw the white devil drilling for Coca-Cola in the Persian Gulf
  —He struck blood tapping the pulse of the capitalist earth

I saw the white devil dusting his crops with the new DDT

The Chornobyl nuclear bomb building pandemonium where Edens lay ravaged & wasted

He's a gringo, a pale-face, honky,
we've blamed him, let's kill him &
start again
let's do something
or get high
yeah, let's get high

I hear the white devil has a new rock to crack—some new smack to smoke—some killer ganja dope to toke—a smooth line of crank to tweek—& a funky big-ass freak with saline tits & a cunt that won't quit

The white devil's a bastard, but he sure knows his shit

THE NOSTALGIA HOUNDS

Scene set (real or painted for movies)
Blackest night invaded by electric gaslamps
Minor Hipsters tadpoles waggling & caviar cool

Making the scene

With the modes & rites of yesterday's Artists:
Yesterday's Major Hepcats

The culture of the NOW: on hold
Waiting for 21st Century science fiction electric orgasms

Our generation borrowed from the past: STYLE
From the twenties to the seventies
On borrowed hair:

> *Crewcut, B∘B, & pompadour, dreadlock, mohawk,*
> *slick back conk // Borrowed shoes, threads, & tunes //*
> *Thrive & shine & drink our booze*

And yet, Art is getting more NAKED
More like the red raw rash on your unwiped ass, VIVID

Reality is not Virtual
Kill your television (before it kills you)

See these creatures, make your own pictures
Wearing (not thrift) but the vintage rags of yesterday's minor too-hip sheepsters & way-way yesterday's poet of lore

I'M NOT AN ARTIST

I'm not an artist
I'm not a poet
I'm not a man
Barely human
Lard progenitor
Consumption engine
Pig slug
Drug bog
Unheeded ethos
Undrunk crank &
Curmudgeon

EMPTY METAPHORS

I'm an empty bottle. A shell on the shore (life moved out). I'm that train wreck cigarette stomped on the sidewalk. A roll of film exposed to the sun. Sightless sockets, a beggar's tin cup. On better days, I'm an apartment for rent, an echo in my belly. I'm clothes outgrown & packed in a dusty garage.

SMASH THE VACUUM TO FREE THE FILAMENT

The professor of poetry rips words at the atomic level
Perfect lines pop like a child in a light bulb factory
thrilled by letting go

Each line
a light bulb
mid-fall
through
space

He drops a thousand

But few resonating with the ideal

A junkie, dropping more more more with diminishing returns

The highs peak fewer & farther

He suffers abstention in the padded cell of his mind

All he can do is think about dropping light bulbs

He can't remember the high or how to find it
in the labyrinth of phrases

He forgets what to write means

Reading student poems, watching tv

He drops tv sets to hear the news break

Waking minutes in the particle accelerator of his mind
fusing word to word

He writes nothing

PASSIONATE PERFORMERS

Let passion take control if you have to take the stage
Let the spirit move as you release the rage

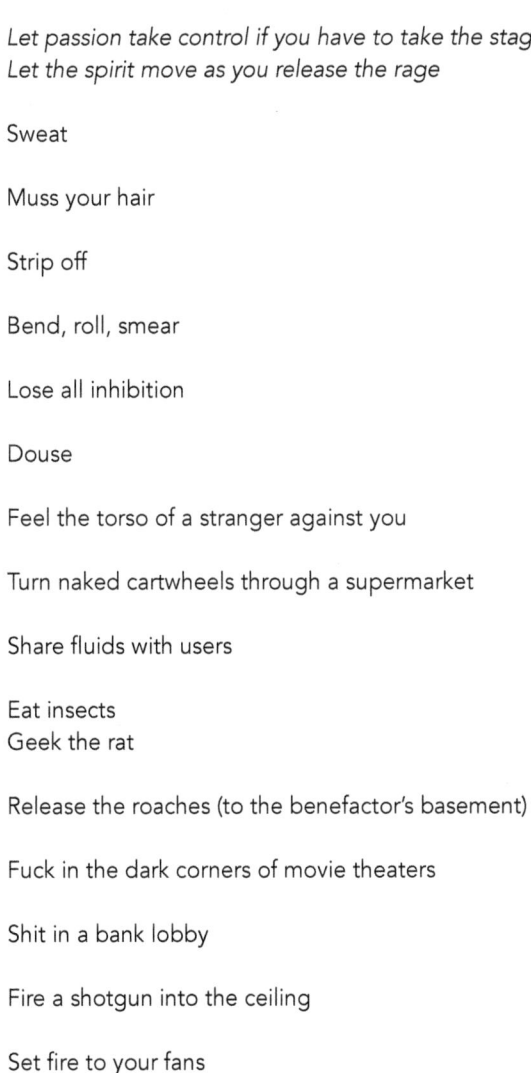

Sweat

Muss your hair

Strip off

Bend, roll, smear

Lose all inhibition

Douse

Feel the torso of a stranger against you

Turn naked cartwheels through a supermarket

Share fluids with users

Eat insects
Geek the rat

Release the roaches (to the benefactor's basement)

Fuck in the dark corners of movie theaters

Shit in a bank lobby

Fire a shotgun into the ceiling

Set fire to your fans

Kill yourself on stage

Nothing a Fire Can't Fix

AFTER WILLAM

So much depends
upon

a black trash can

laying on its side near the Watts Tower

"No 3 Strikes"

painted in dripping yellow letters

A JIMMY JAZZ POEM

On stage
I touched the lips of young ladies watching &
held Bugaloo finger-glasses over the eyes to illustrate my line

    Big I understand honey eyes &
        kicked over the monitor
            falling
                    off
                            the stage

rolling   *around*

   floor   *on the*

r e e l i n g a n d s e e ming
                      drunk
                      teething on angry
              one chord per emotion driven music
                    spinning
      in my inadequate sea

  CRAZY
                I'm screaming at them

BEES

Einstein may or may not have said something like,

"If the bees disappeared, we'd have four years to live."

Does this sound right?
I mean, why **four** years?
And when did Einstein study entomology?

There were plenty of creatures before bees evolved

Even plants
So when the news reported
last week that hundreds of millions of bees
in North America
had vanished,
I wasn't alarmed
for the amoebæ

ANGELA

I feel like screaming your name. I want you to fuck me in front of the window without shame without shame—our love your shawl. Angela, suckle my horny penis while I write the words of our coupled joy for the literate world to share. Angela, listen & tell truths to me & dance me around & never let me sleep without creating something even if its only a passionate moment. Angela, come kiss me & let us be one—one force driving to freedom pan-ultimate & let us experience without the moral constraint of sheep & let us not be just sheep ourselves, we will fuse something eternal & grow it up beyond popular conception to a realm of truth & beauty & lies & love & hate SO BE IT, Angela, we will steal the heart-shaped Cupid's crown from Juliet & Romeo those love novices who shriveled under strife. For it is more difficult to live with love & its offspring than to shrivel at the dagger's hilt or drink death in a vile mockery of love I call it paltry in comparison to my heart which beats for you, my feet which grow beat for you, my back which breaks for you & my cock which aches for you. For my soul which is you, Angela. If my expectations are delusion, walk away; seek complacency & I will re-invent myself in the lowest bowels of tragedy. I won't die like a boyish Romeo though the urge & motive be furtive. I will finger fuck myself with the nubs of nerveless knuckles & create out of friction alone if I must. I will tear the ears off my head with dull knives & paint god with the bloody cartilage swabs of sound while she plays the drums which roll out in time: Boom boom boom boom—Satan, Buddha & all the followers of Malcolm X can tear at the bass strings of my Promethean gut which will captivate all in a cum-swallowing whirl of mad bliss & when the sun goes out & fate illuminates the carcass of this world with the nostalgia of our love, I will laugh like the time you threw sand in my face at the beach & I will eat sand for the sake of glorious contempt, my new steamy mistress. I will spring myself on the reincarnated Angela & together we will invade the stony gravel graves of time & love & together mix the death kool aid—then when my last white hairs choke of drought & scream for your ancient afternoon (not morning) breath, I too will find peace like Romeo & You & Juliet & Our Love

Nothing a Fire Can't Fix

GRAMMAR

A verb is a noun

AFTER EMILY

Beauty, death, love, & happiness
written on a slip of paper
fit in my pocket

DUMPSTER

Sleeping in a Tuesday-pick-up-dumpster
It's Monday, I think

There's garbage all around,
but my mind blocks the…

TRAPS

Set traps for your future self

JONAS SALK

Jonas Salk
is dead
heart failure

One of the great scientific minds having said,

> "When you hear the clop of hooves behind you,
> don't guess zebra."

Sound bite about his polio vaccine & work on AIDS

Two minutes

A FIRE

It was cold & dark
until I built a fire &
decided to live here

Nothing a Fire Can't Fix

SHALL I COMPARE THEE SUNDAY DRIVE?

Is the peacock not a little uneasy? Robert Walser

- Cold peanuts

- Clothes

- Books

- A Sunday drive

- Feeding animals in the zoo

- The men in prison too

- A winter sunset resplendent over the sea

- Clear Lake

- A small house, a green lawn, a crystal blue pool out back… even a small cottage with a sound roof

- My daughter playing soccer in her new uniform

- All that mother might have been

- My health

- Rearing to cum…?

- Better poets in lonely rooms steal time in broom closets to write the sublime next steps in the human text

THE FLEAS I'VE KILLED

The pacifist shows the will to murder
hidden behind lofty sentiment

    Humanity

When push comes to the edge, I kill

ESPRESSO EX MACHINA

The ghost in the machine is caffeine

AMPUTATION

My grandma ended a story
about both my aunt & her son, my cousin,
in hospital to have limbs amputated
with the phrase: god is good

I end the story about this legless aunt & armless cousin
with the phrase: god damn

SPY

Neighbor stands outside a kitchen door, away from her family. She stares at the empty alley. Her face piled heavy into one hand leaning, dejected, on the chain link. I'm above, looking out/spying from the bathroom window. I'd like to touch her thick black hair. She appears to be pregnant. A girl beckons her into the house. She moves to the door, disappears.

LA POSTA

There was a guy at La Posta (the taco shop) sleeping in a wheelchair in a shady spot. He had one leg & one arm. His bald skull was scabbed & blistered. He was dirty. His one hand was calloused & pink & the pores were inky black. His arm stump was dirty. While we ordered bean burritos, he peed leaving a puddle under the wheelchair. We watched the urine soak into the dragging empty flap of his corduroy jeans.

UNTITLED

You can't free the slave in your heart,
until you kill the cop in your mind

PINBALL FIXATION

Pinball is nihilism—the destruction of time & money

Cecil & I spend our cash, playing quarter after quarter, on this game of skill terrorized by moments of bad luck

Forgetting to sip each his pint of the black

When that necessary ball arcs down the drain eluding control, I shout curse words & shove the machine like I want to fight it

Pinball is about the limits of control

That it fortifies the liver while raising the blood pressure, saving as it maims—a paradox resolved

balance, catch, pass

We found a spirituality we could stomach in the "magic" manipulation of the silver ball

like monks staring at a wall
like minimalists after the fire

BELIEF

Scientists don't believe,
they test hypotheses

String theory,
so far,
has been
untestable

You might say

Nothing is true,
since
everything,
so far,
has proven
wrong

THE IMPOSSIBILITY OF AN ANTI-BANANA POEM

Writing an anti-banana poem is just bananas
This anti-banana poem got ruined by the word..banana

"Big Mike, where are you?"

The despotic pink fist of monoculture could hit you
the way it strikes the bloated tummy of un niño de la finca
but the news (torture, poverty, malnutrition…) dissipates in the
 sweet ripe fragrance

Extinction creeping across the world like fungus can't stop
breakfast

These lines decry the worst blue-black, rotten, stinking, filthy
banana clutched like a dildo in a deathhand
crawling with larvae you didn't see but tasted
leads you to believe that bananas are hell

which makes them dangerous & cool &
misunderstood & full of mystery—an adventure

Even people who don't eat bananas will tell you they are glorious

Peeled before frozen & whipped like iced cream
Bananas walk through the American dream like a bunch of giraffes
through tall grass

A white bowl of red strawberries
vividly red right through the bite
smelling like a summer rain-washed morning after clouds have
lifted & dripping juice down the chin
onto her belly laugh in bed as she greedily swipes one more than
her share leaving the empty white bowl

might have been a lovely anti-banana poem
until named

DESIRÉ SAID

Desiré said: I met this bum in front of the taco shop & he said he was hungry & could I give him money to buy food. So, in the taco shop, I got an extra taco for the bum, had the clerk put it in a separate bag, came out, gave it to the bum, & he said,

What's this?

You said you were hungry.

I don't want this shit!
        He slammed it to the gutter.

Well, stand in front of the bank, fool.

PICK UP MILK ON A BEER RUN?

Baby eating Kix in watery chocolate milk
because we haven't gone to the store for
anything but beer

A GOOD HEART

My dad once told me
that I had a good heart, but
a sick & twisted mind

Even at the time, I worried
it wasn't twisted enough

ASHTRAY

For several years, on my way to work, I walked passed a woman who made a camp on Broadway, downtown.

She was organized, with clothes folded & stacked squarely in a handcart. She sat on a blue tarpaulin spread out against moisture from below & when she smoked, she sat with her back to the street facing a chain link fence tapping the gray ash from her cigarette into a ceramic ashtray.

NOSTALGIC ROCK

I remember when punk was a safety pin jammed thru your cheek
WHEN Iggy Stooge dove into the crowd smeared with peanut butter

WHEN only 1000 people owned a Velvet Underground record
WHEN kids from NY City rolled around in glass at CBGB's
WHEN Johnny Rotten spit in your face & refused to lip-sync on Bandstand

WHEN girls didn't want to be pretty
WHEN music came on vinyl
WHEN Patti Smith pissed in a river
WHEN Debby Harry was in Playboy
WHEN you had to drive to Santa Monica to get Dr. Martens
WHEN disco sucked
WHEN Jello Biafra socked you for jumping on stage
WHEN Mike Ness fell down the stairs
WHEN Black Flag, the Circle Jerks, Adolescents, Fear, the Minutemen, & China White played the Stardust Ballroom

WHEN the Germs told their friends to bring food
WHEN Joey said, "We're not students, we're the Ramones."
WHEN The Clash was on Fridays
WHEN Fear was on Saturday Night Live
WHEN Jake Burns said, "Hanx!"
WHEN Toy Dolls refused to play a gymnasium
WHEN H.R. flipped 360 degrees landing on his feet & the Bad Brains started a riot

WHEN John & Exene sang, *She had to leave... Los Angeles*
WHEN Butthole Surfers were banned in nine states
WHEN three kids came to school with mohawks after The Decline
WHEN Youth Brigade played at The Palisades Roller Rink
that's now a condominium

WHEN The Misfits played the Adams Avenue theater

that's now a Yarn Barn

WHEN a Suicidal Boy jumped off the 35-foot PA at the Olympic
WHEN "Exploited, UK Subs, Dr. Know" remained on the marquee
of a condemned theater for five years

WHEN Tim Maze told the Filipino-American-Veterans-Association
he was renting their hall for "a dance"

WHEN the bouncers tried to stop us to photographing Joan Jett
while she sang a Buzzcocks tune at the fair

WHEN Social Spit put me on the guest list for life & broke up a
week later

WHEN I pushed my father's buttons so hard, he threw that can of
beer at me

WHEN Ministry of Truth played our living room
WHEN the furniture began to break
WHEN the walls began to sweat
WHEN they wouldn't let Angelic Upstarts in the country
WHEN the cops call to shut down our punk rock picnic was
answered with rocks & bottles

WHEN mad Mark Rude beat the shit out of some hippies &
lit their house on fire

WHEN the Masque closed
WHEN the Tool & Die closed
WHEN The Casbah closed
WHEN Sid OD'd
WHEN Darby Crash OD'd
WHEN Johnny Thunders was murdered
WHEN Mia Zapata was murdered
WHEN Stiv Bators was hit by a car
WHEN Kurt Kobain blew his own head off with a shotgun &
Nirvana finally made sense

Nothing a Fire Can't Fix

WALKING PAST THE CHURCH

A gust of wind blew out of the church
catching up & lifting your skirt,
so god could see your panties

MMMMMMMM

I was ummmmmmmm
thinking
that my life
my blood hair veins
limbs
didn't have mmmmmmeaning without you &
thinking still & always thinking
that what mmmmeaning we have is
fleeting

PRESIDENTS

Presidents, you might think,
would end in prison more
than start there

URBAN LEGEND

A fiction by Kenneth Anger

Fame, money, attention, love
An art deco bath
A failed marriage
An unwanted pregnancy

Manic depression

Champagne tile at Mr. A's
The pool at The Lafayette

Sleeping pills ingested
Make-up applied, hair styled
You should be in pictures

Pubic hairs shaved in the shape of a heart

Lay me down to die nude on satin sheets

Flowers ordered & arranged

A portrait of beauty in death… until

puke upchuck vomit
gut wrench retch—Do it in the toilet
Run to the toilet

Run Run Run

Slip… in a pool of vomit

Crack

Busted skull on pink porcelain
sink into a toilet headfirst & drown

Nothing a Fire Can't Fix

WHEN THE NEIGHBOR GETS SHOT

When I hear gunshots, I think it's the neighbor's TV or an old car backfiring

When the police arrive followed by the camera
time stops like a photograph from the Third World

Outside, yellow caution tape provides color as the setting sun leaves everything gray, inside, I imagine red like the lips on a Hollywood actress

The asshole with the microphone calls it news
After sunset, cop cars & news trucks are beacons

We wait as men deliberate

A cop wants you to make a statement, but you don't know why people shoot each other

The kids cry in the alley with shit in their pants, you say
 Well… once, but their faces are always dirty & screaming, someone was always shouting

> Fuck you bitch
>> You bastard fuck you

They were neighbors: couples fight, come & go with groceries, play the TV too loud too late

We called child protective services, a neighbor says

Police, ambulance, camera leave with less flash & haste

A few days on, the new neighbors carry in clothes on hangers from the back of their car

You hope they won't ask about the stain on the carpet

WE ARE HERE

Plumes of methane
on Mars
could mean tiny life
even now
groping in the dirt
beneath the surface of the red planet

Farting out their existence

  We are here

        We Live

                We Consume

         We Reproduce

HUMANITY

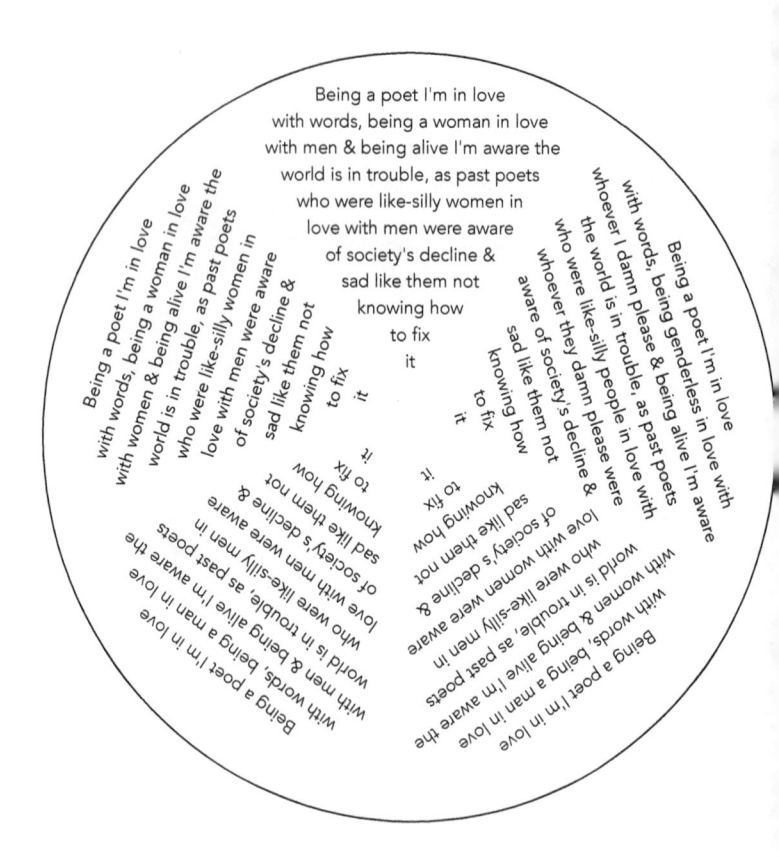

Being a poet I'm in love with words, being a woman in love with men & being alive I'm aware the world is in trouble, as past poets who were like-silly women in love with men were aware of society's decline & sad like them not knowing how to fix it

Being a poet I'm in love with words, being a woman in love with women & being alive I'm aware the world is in trouble, as past poets who were like-silly women in love with men were aware of society's decline & sad like them not knowing how to fix it

Being a poet I'm in love with words, being genderless in love with whoever I damn please, being alive I'm aware the world is in trouble, as past poets who were like-silly people in love with whoever they damn please were aware of society's decline & sad like them not knowing how to fix it

Being a poet I'm in love with words, being a man in love with men & being alive I'm aware the world is in trouble, as past poets who were like-silly men in love with men were aware of society's decline & sad like them not knowing how to fix it

Being a poet I'm in love with words, being a man in love with women & being alive I'm aware the world is in trouble, as past poets who were like-silly men in love with women were aware of society's decline & sad like them not knowing how to fix it

JOHNNY THUNDERS WAS MURDERED

What's that ringing sound?

We heard the last song from a man who died alone
kicking the junk, methadone
needle in the toilet, New Orleans

Feel the guitar, feel what it means

Junkie gangsters robbed his stash
Cut off his head, stole his cash

You can't stop the music in the underworld
Can't put your arms around the memory of a girl

Recognize sunken white flesh
crawling Bourbon after a late-night sesh
(spot a hungry junkie by weazle eye)
Follow em to da room, light bulb swaying,
bottle-o-water on a table & one chair

Half an old lemon dried in the fridge &
spike up an o.d.

That's how it ends
How we lose friends

junk junk junkie Oh Johnny

Sad love sad songs &
universal call-to-dance guitar
in the wasted underbelly of 60s strung-out pop
Dolls, Heartbreaking, so low
Dirty Johnny from Queens
Hello Death, a darkened room, in New Orleans

Nothing a Fire Can't Fix

UNREQUITED LOVE

Imagine a human so beautiful
she'd never known unrequited love

Everyone loves her or wants to

The attentions of the pawing
humanity

The abrasion of Paparazzi

In 1983, a friend who was smart & shy & sweet & sincere & honest sent his first love letter & got his first rejection

"I do not reciprocate your feelings"

ELEGY FOR JIM

The elegist should know more of a moon or a man than its gibbous phase. Anonymous

A screaming came across the sky
on Broadway two hours after sunrise

A black crow darted before the cityscape
a small hawk in pursuit of his tail feathers…
reminding me, strangely, of conversations
in a teacher's lounge at a language school
in San Diego with our friend Jim Ricker

Jim

Hippie Jim, parsing the spoken words of his interlocutors,
asking each to think & re-think before speaking

The talons of his sharp logic clipping some who dared use
anecdotal evidence to support a claim

Hippie Jim, there was a fry cook in your heart & a prescriptive
grammar Snoot

A fry cook flipping hotcakes in a Sunday rush at The Big Kitchen

Hippie Jim with your Master's degree, where is your long hair now?

A fry cook who never minced words & a usage cop with an
etymologist's nightstick upside the head of the Green Grocer—
"Who does he think he is with his 10 Items or Less sign?"

Hippie Jim, you old polemicist, you coot
never angry, but always ready & able to argue

   EVERYTHING

Nothing a Fire Can't Fix

Hippie Jim, with your long hair, were you a Marxist? Can you explain Marx's Labor Theory of Value one more time?

You old union man, you Wobblie, you Uber-hater

We'll kick hell out of any scab that crosses your picket line

Hippie Jim, why were you shaking your fist
at the lack of common sense in the Ottoman Empire
over coffee with the muse?

Yer cantankerous-misanthropic-curmudgeon mask
didn't fool the people you loved
A circus tent couldn't mask a heart like that

Hippie Jim, will they bury you in bolo tie & seersucker coat?

Will your hair be long in heaven?

Will you give Jesus a piece of your mind?

Will God pour you a beer & with a slap on the back say, "Good Job Buddy?"

Hippie Jim, you could be sober a thousand years, or a thousand lonely nights & all your courage & conviction wouldn't stop us finger-waggers from waving your final vices like a red flag—

Did you really eat a 7-11 chili dog & chocolate milk every fucking day?

Any man who can find joy in the grit in the bottom of a styrofoam cup of Folger's can be happy in this world

O, secret joy teacher

Ask your students to seize the day
tap your enthusiasm in class & field trips

to places they have never been
 Jim, Hippie Jim

You Teacher
You Reader

Who will speak at length about the great writers of our time?

   Who will follow Pynchon & Bill Vollmann?

   Who will read Edward Abbey's FBI file & care about David Foster Wallace?

   Who will throw his body on the gears of the capitalist machine & wonder in what desert Edward Abbey lies?

Jim

You teacher
You Reader
You Study-hard
You Knower (of so many things)
History dies with a man like you
History falls into the memory hole

Jim

You Knower
You Carer
You Talker

Your hawk soars above the tower
the crow counts his days

POEM TO A MORMON FATHER

This is the cock I put inside your daughter like a sweaty sock hanging limp, but excited as a stream of bright yellow urine pours into the piss pot

This is the cock she's sucked

The balls are sweaty, the way she rolls them in her mouth like pearls glisten with saliva, a jewel held up to the light

Inside, descendants of the seed she's swallowed with her womb the tomb where orgasms go to die

This is the penis she's gripped with fingers with teeth

This is the shriveled version of the member that set birth in action

Produced fruit

A grand-daughter, all smiles & curls, who doesn't carry on your belief system

It must be hard on you, this mix of joy & disappointment

The latent wish that some cock besides this blasphemous poet's resided where you put your faith

VODKA TONIC

A preference for harder liquor sprouts with a twisted lime

I don't drink beer anymore. Forget those schooners at the Alibi.

It's about vodka
  with tonic at NuNu's, in a bloody Mary at The Jewel Box
It's about gin

       a pitcher of martinis at Vesuvio

Rye Manhattans

At a time when my friends are trying to get sober, I'm learning the fine science of drinking

BOTTLE O WINE

Bottle O wine
Bottle O wine

I can sing your praises, through dark & sunny ages

Bottle O wine

Bom Bomp

It's 9:31 & GOOD NEWS

The wine is gone & I have successfully walked
to the corner store for more
dodging drug dealer, gang bangers, &
a drunk who rolled his vehicle onto the sidewalk

I'M NOT A SCIENTIST

dilettante
poetaster
layman
barely sentient
ignorant of calculus
algebraically challenged
tone-deaf
—black hole
—division by zero
—quantum gravity

PERTURBATIVE APPROACH

I seldom found the right spot to rub her,
on finding couldn't seem to stay on
long enough, so I rub all around the pubic bone
leaving her clitoris, at least, perturbed

QUANTUM MECHANIC

Oppenheimer, that
grease monkey,
couldn't fix my car

THE RED JEANS

I swore an oath to wear the same pants for 2 weeks & 3 days. They went from clean stiff to soft-sagging, droopy drawers. You mocked me. Scoffed at me. Denigrated my desire to go easy on the laundry. I changed undies every 3 days. Changed socks 5 times. I showered, shaved & shit 7 times, but didn't fuck even once. I wore them to the nightclub, where they came back smoky. I wore them to the mountains: where they climbed hills, boulders, & trees. I wore them to the nightclub (a 2nd time) where they came back even smokier. I wore them to the movies, in the sick bed 3 days inert. I took them off at night for sleeping because they cramp that morning boner. I wore the **RED JEANS** to a used bookstore. To walk the dog. The **RED JEANS** with the 'hipster merit badge' chain wallet dangling & studded leather belt cinching the waist. The **RED JEANS** with the union label. The **RED JEANS** saw the sun set & the sky scream like a sore pink tonsil. The **RED JEANS** heard Ginsberg chant with The Clash 8 times on cassette. The **RED JEANS** played pinball, the **RED JEANS** got drunk, the **RED JEANS**... the **RED JEANS** ... [Any attempt at a Marxist interpretation of the red jeans may reveal the violence inherent in the system.] The **RED JEANS** chauffeured Angela to work & skipped through the woods to grandma's house. They crafted gifts to place under The Midwinter Festival Tree after refusing to go shopping. They starred in a student film & danced jumped hopped They didn't hump & are still waiting to be unzipped by adept fingers. The **RED JEANS** love me & I love them (like that velveteen rabbit story I read my daughter at bedtime). The **RED JEANS**, the **RED JEANS**, feverish mad ugly poet jeans & me running around the city with uncombed hair & a crucifix up my ass. The **RED JEANS** sat in outdoor cafes & purchased bean burritos at midnight. The **RED JEANS** read 5 books in 3 days. The **RED JEANS** licked & fucked pussy in dreams, wet dreams, dry dreams, the wet jeans talked red heat to a madman prophet about god. The **RED JEANS** heard the voice of god: "Don't part with the red jeans. Extend your vacation beyond eternity to the here & now. Wear the red jeans until they grow holy, then burn them in a fire, a pyre, as the heroes of your viking ancestry."

Nothing a Fire Can't Fix

Sea-faring jeans   land-roving jeans   tree-swinging jeans
fish-catching fruit-picking nut-gathering sky-groping jeans
monkey brain jeans because evolution ain't nothing but
the recombination of atomic matter

Big bang spun relative jeans into a universe: The Great Dying, The
Great Bleaching, The Great Depression (aka the bell bottom years),
The Great Pegging, The Tight Ass Decade, The Great Sagging, &
The Great Lowering

Hey low pants move your sweet ass back to high school

Brittany Spears' jeans are 99.9% the same as James Dean's jeans

coffee drinking pill poppin gin gulping TV watching jeans:
My **RED JEANS** saw Green Day on MTV 30 times in 2 days
my magic jeans, my cow, my red I'll wear them 'til they're dead…
JEANS

THE FREE WAY

41,000 Killed
An invidious enemy that can't be seen
But WE declare war
The cars must be stopped
Bomb Detroit
Sanctions on Tokyo

41,000 traffic deaths per year
on US soil

War
War

DENIAL

I'm not angry.
I'm not white.
I'm not male.

I'm not privileged.

CONSERVATION

I've pissed
four times in the toilet
without flushing

Nothing a Fire Can't Fix

IN THE STUDIO

A dungeon without windows
painting relief from memory or imagination
for inspiration
                —bring sounds on tape
exotic incense
to catapult mind-travel over unforeseen battlements

Dance to the sound of your own nudity

Songs sung to please the self &
reading the song of myself

Carry in ideas & raw penned emotion
with borrowed books

Measure time by heartbeat

You can't age if you don't count the days
 But the mirror &
my nails need cutting &
 hair at my hip

The artist is never alone with his work

GRANNY

"Those are Euryops, some kind of god damn daisy."

"If America needed an enema, Duluth is the place they'd stick it in."

"She doesn't know shit from Shinola. I don't care if she drinks, as long as she can stand up."

"This wheel chair is a pain in the ass."

"Scottsdale is a plastic phony little town."

Granny licks Vicodin, crushed by her daughter with a rolling pin, off a sheet of wax paper. A spot of chalky white powder coats the tip of her elongated nose.

The closed room is thick with nicotine. It's time to lift her off the davenport, into the wheelchair, out of the wheelchair, onto the toilet.

She's got an ugly dog, called Nubbins, that growls at the messenger from the Library of the Blind, they understand each other.

The care provider has gone for a bottle of rye.

"These books on tape are mostly crap. Dickens knew how to develop a character. DH Lawrence, James Joyce: I've got no use for those two."

"When I was a young nurse in World War II, the colonel gave me a copy of Ulysses & I thought, What's all the fuss?"

"Hemingway was a real man. None of this Pollyanna shit."

Nothing a Fire Can't Fix

CHIAPAS 45

Chiapas 45 Chiapas 45 Chiapas 45 (Kosovo 45)

I am the oppressor & the oppressed

but don't ever call me repressor or repressed because
I believe in speaking freely & do so

I am the oppressor & the oppressed

Living in a crazy mixed-up stone soup of poverty & affluence
I have things that I don't need which is the definition of filthy rich,
yet most of my clothes are hand-me-downs,
yet the furniture I sit on has been handed DOwn

I am the oppressor & the oppressed

Seeing so many folks **without** the things they need to be
H-A-P-P-Y (I hear their babies cry for want)
I leave worn clothes & applied appliances &
played-with toys on the sidewalk & think I'm doing my part

I spent a day among normal folks recently
realized I no longer speak their language

They seem to me like filler, or fog, like that styrofoam popcorn
inside the great cardboard box of the earth

In San Diego we've got a 14-million-dollar fence
(me foolish enough to do away with borders)
Mr. styrofoam-popcorn-soul America got a 14-million-dollar fence
The poets & the peace activists got one too
Until we dig a hole or provide a safe house for the weary

I'm not afraid to lose the little bit I have, yet, regret that I don't
have the *juevos* to be the good *coyote* in the new underground
railroad bringing the slaves of circumstance to the pursuit of

happiness

I am the oppressor & the oppressed

I stuff my face at the buffet // I don't leave a mess for the busboy

I sleep comfortably in hotel beds // I clean up for the maid

I spend all day lallygagging on fresh-cut grass // I know who cut it

I drink until I get drunk // I can't rationalize that

I fuck shit up // because shit needs to be fucked up

Nothing a Fire Can't Fix

THE JOHNSON FAMILY

Tamara Johnson, poet, asleep
in a Lawrence, Kansas fleabag motel

Having hidden in the back seat of the car
while Angela & I checked in to save four bucks

All bitching & grumbling, we grow disgust
with naked habits

Jazz grates your ears…

Baroness of the highway driving madly on our rattle-bone chariot
crushing the transmission teeth in excess of
$$\text{SPEED} \times \text{TIME} = \text{DISTANCE}$$
The closet
close
proximity
of 13 days in a car

The nerves are rubber tires exposing
the steel fibers of the grey matter
grinding teeth to powder

Screeching against inequity from the stage
whence does that pain arise?

Who hurt you?

When you hurt Angela, it was my fault
like a croquet ball struck by a hammer

In Tulsa, I had to get out &
your line of poetry

Across three lanes of traffic
fit like genius

You won't let the professors tell you how to write, any more than you'd let another woman gnaw on your chicken boy after lickin' your lips,

We didn't need attention until it wasn't offered

The spam-eating mob drag racing & burning garbage

We suffered ennui
on vacation
in America

No step taken for mankind, no leap

Pointless mouse chase pointed out

To hear us laugh, you'd think pleasure was our objective

Running from in guise of seeking
Pleasure flies by night, evanescent

You pull the musty sheet over your head, sensitive to light, while an unfamiliar spider spins its web in the wash-up

STUCKISM

I had a student who said: Principles are the opposite of Intelligence.

I caught his meaning while finding vice-principals more abhorrent.

In 9th grade, there was a teacher with long hair rumored to smoke dope with the stoners. By senior year, he'd cut his hair short & started wearing a suit.

> "I like to reinvent myself every seven years."

Copernicus & Galileo recanted.
Giordano Bruno was burned at the stake.

I used to think Mediocrities was a Greek philosopher.

TV? School? Marriage? Work?

It's easier to carry a NO BLOOD 4 OIL sign at the protest than to give up your car.

a) A poetry reading is a conduit of affirmation (like television)
b) A poem should challenge what you believe
c) none of the above

Imagine a proscenium where words launch like a coward launches a cruise missile.

Social Einstein-ism: Quarks of affirmation pass through our bodies. An unexpected neutrino takes the form of a girl child stepping on a land mine; a stray dog trots off with a limb while the village burns. It's our fault. Your fault, my fault.

We fed that dog.

Who discovered America?
Whose independence was won from King George?
Why did we fight a civil war?
The Spanish-American War?
The Mexican-American War?
What if Japan had a military base in Seattle to protect their national interest?

How many people were killed in the Vietnam War?

I looked up Manifest Destiny in the thesaurus & saw a picture of genocide.

You are like a black flea on the rim of a white toilet bowl.

Whipped with your own bootstraps, a slave to things.

The bums are at the beach.

Throw a picnic at the fault line where the first & third worlds rub together.

An earthquake takes a few lives, so we sentence Mother Earth to death?

We once believed in the death penalty, but the planet is not guilty.

Stuckism for Dummies

Section #1 Our values keep us from changing
Section #2 People can change (even if you don't like the result)
Section #3 The flat earth society
Section #4 Overcoming indoctrination
Section #5 Question institutions as well as specific actions
Section #6 Is art an agent of change or an affirmation of values?
Section #7 Poetry readings mostly feature affirmation
Section #8 Questions where the common answer is a lie
Section #9 Revaluation of values: Earth is the new bottom line

Nothing a Fire Can't Fix

NEWTON'S SLEEP

Do you have faith in history?
Do you have faith in science?

Political science would be an oxymoron,
if Acton's maxim weren't true.

Your dogma is more dogmatic than a dog's… dogma.

A dog will return to the spot where he found food,
but after a few days famine will change his mind.

When confronted with new & better information, act.

BEAUTY = SYMMETRY

A physicist might say beauty is symmetry, but
I don't care if one breast is larger

DRUNK BLUES

I showed up drunk to my AA meeting
eleven guys with a problem just like mine

We smoke packs of cigarettes
shades pulled low like sleepy eyelids shutting

Telling sunken tales about
  rotting liver
  shaking hands &
  the last blank spot

I listen without speaking UNTIL
my turn?

A pretty thought of alcohol jumped up to my slur tongue
disguised as a party girl
with open smile
free-floating in my brain
like the disappearing landscape in front of the wheel

With big I UNDERSTAND HONEY eyes &
lips too busy waiting for a kiss
to speak truth about what she sees inside

Instead of My name is Jimmy Jazz & I'm an alcoholic
I said I'm Jimmy Jazz & I love to drink
Beer clouds my brain, it stops the think
I love to be drunk on words & women

(My voice gets creepy here, it crouches)

Drunk where music is a spinning cell
in my vein & brain jail
spinning me another tale
of the low road to high times

Nothing a Fire Can't Fix

I don't care if I sleep through the sunrise
as long as the moon shines &
the city lights blaze on the dark bay water &
time can slip through the bottle noose
into the sewer stomach of street sleeping sore whores

As long as the bass beat drum hump
ferments into the jang jang guitar slang
under the scratchy throat whine
in the downtown jump joint

I wanted them to think I was crazy—different—
possessed by spirits, but eleven heads nodded &
the next mouth opened to speak

PIAF

I'm in love
with an eclectic ritual
embodied in a roaring
jazz goddess

Tea & Tom Waits in the morning
bread & brie cheese our repast
heady talk & kisses
swinging through bands soaked in vodka tonic Bacchanals
then huddling under the open city window
feeling full the presence & gravity of mystery
pressing at the innards men have called soul

AN IDEA

Boys pee outside

IDENTITY ZERO

Identity crisis skinhead, confusion rules your mind

i am so vapid sucked clean of me
been searching magazine articles
on Gen X for a new

      i...dent...i...ty!

Recalled the old drinking beer after beer sot-brained
Seymour F. McBean, changin' on into the wolfman,
punishing an identity thief
a half-decade back
after the dude copied the hair, the clothes, the music...the style
with one last sip fly-at-your-skull beer bottle

Punk-u-ation.

TELL THE REVOLUTIONARY COURT TO HANG THE METERPIGS FIRST

A New Guernica for Colin Powell who had Picasso's tapestry covered 5 February 2003 before delivering a call to war

I feel the dry fibers on my fingertips as I stretch the noose around his neck, I will murder myself into history, change something (if only the roster of the living)

A hero in the streets, a good-looking white urban terrorist, the Elvis of looters & arsonists

This bastard wrote me a parking ticket, but now I have him by the hair

C'mere kid, shimmy this cell tower. Yes, toss the rope … Stop kicking me. Why? Why? You are the international symbol for wrong.

I threw food on the sidewalk & they killed for me. I promised that one a six-pack to slit a rich man's throat & she did it with his car keys singing:

> Class war, rich vs poor, they wouldn't let us up,
> so we'll bring em to the floor

> Class war, rich vs poor, they wouldn't let us up,
> so we'll bring em to the floor

When I get on TV, I'm going to reach out of the set & yank you off the couch, rip your entrails & whip you across the eyes

Kill every stupid fuck that I can

I am the shepherd. The butcher. The Cleanser [Call me Ajax]

Nothing a Fire Can't Fix

I'm inertia come to kill your ideals

Pull him up… The cameras… Spit on your hands & slick your hair.
People think you're crazy when you smile with blood on your face.
Hold that rope… The cops won't be here 'til the commercial break;
they're giving tickets to jaywalkers man

A balding curmudgeon holds a Zippo to his pant leg

Three homeless men hold rolled newspapers like torches
The sun sets on the foot of Broadway like a ripe orange
Sirens echo among the buildings

Here they come

Riot cops charge with black sticks; bums pelt them with coins
Heads split; I see the spilt brains of soldiers on the asphalt

Run

When standers by point at me, they point at themselves

Jackboots click a rhythm // Legs run // Mouths scream // A horse
bites at the broken spear stuck in his ass

Scream

Sirens & car horns & the sobs of individuals rise
The tear gas seems redundant

A black male grabs a cop's .38

Saigon Penn!

The blood countess bathes in the killing fields

A homeless soldier sinks scattered teeth in a cop's cheek // I see
the chunk of flesh like a puzzle-piece in a madman's blackened
gums

The smell of burning human flesh excites madness in the hungry

A man with a cracked skull, unlike a baby seal, has the constitution or stupidity to cup his brains

Two cops kick the shit out of that woman who pushes her cart down Fifth Avenue

She's my mother!

She's been dead, but they continue pounding her through frustration

Swing for the pretty teeth of dental plans

The warm summer asphalt smells dirty

The meterpig swings: his flesh, our flag
I see fortresses with bloody human banners waving

> Kill the metermaids // Hang them from the
> streets // Stuff tickets in their enflamed anuses
> & light them on fire // Peel their faces & mock
> dance with skin mask, twitch & burn inside, like
> the flag mocking the wind

A cop bludgeons someone above me. I tie his shoelaces together as blood drips on my hair. He's beaten the skull off a corpse. Head & torso fall to the street. He falls, I'm on him like a rat, straddling his chest. He's exhausted from beating & screaming. I reach into his eye socket scoop the retina. It looks good. I rub the goo of eye into his face. Thumb it in his nostril.

He sp-sp-spits bubbling crude

Power America's cars with blood
The Gulf War was a game show

Nothing a Fire Can't Fix

Oglala braves scalp the corpses, don the uniforms, & dance for the spirits

Smashing glass // Bank alarms // Sirens // The creaking moan of atrophied steel

A yell from the chaos: Thanks be to god!

A rivulet of blood, bile, & urine trickles to the gutter
We do have efficient storm drains

Thanks be to god

OUR INSIDE-OUT LOVE STORY

I'm no longer horny
My sex-rapacious consciousness
has changed again
shed its skin
my cock is a snake
winding around the naked delicacy of young thighs, I strike
but it's my tongue, my mouth, my face
devouring your pussy, drowning in it
your wet lips hydrate my passion
I stretch the lips over my face & wriggle my way inside
once the shoulders are in, it's easy...
almost drowning in your viscera
'til mouth kisses a lung
taking your breath at the wellspring
tasting the back of your nipples as I slink on up
my brain in your brain
my heart in your heart
my erect cock shooting jism out of your vagina from the inside
fucking you from the uterus outward
my arms in your arms
my hands in your hands
our eyes
our noses
our lips, kissing inside-out instead of outside-in
our hair
our hips
our inside-out love story
our tears
our years
our sexually transmitted infections
our grave
our dirty old bones turning to dust, together

A STUDENT

A student wanted to write a book
about his mistakes, so
others could learn from them

Everyone writes that book;
no one reads it

FISHING

Give a man a fish & you feed him for a day
Teach man to fish & he'll empty the ocean

THE CAT LEAPS

The cat leaps
on the chair
licks my toes
        this a poem
embodied or rendered important by the loud, extra loud, ticks
of the clock as time runs out

OLD HEAD

minerva, Gail, Old Head from Philly
I keep the photo of You with BB King
close

You split fast
I miss you

Wish I had a flask
brimmed with your suave timing
for the line

People should know how close you got
to Mingus, with Sun Ra living next door, & Lester Bowie
How close to Miss Brooks, consultant of letters
when you worked at The National Geographic
They should see that photo of You with Jayne Cortez

You ran with Kool

I don't know why some poets "make it"
or even what it means for a poet to make it
I don't know why some poets make it &
why some poets die alone

Some poets who make it die alone
old friend, I guess we all die alone

They put Zora Hurston's body in an unmarked grave, after all
At least I could visit Ms. Angela in the Hope
Sit on the grass, think about her, & all she would have become

On my Facebook feed, the memorial I wrote for you got
33 hearts 24 thumbs up 21 hugs & 2 tears

SOCIAL EINSTEINISM

There's no one smart enough to write this poem.

Einstein wasted 30 years looking for an equation to reconcile the behavior of galaxies & the forces binding atomic particles.

It's taken me 30 years to square
the behavior of the individual to society.

$$e = \pm mc2$$
———————————

Do What Thou Wilt

Einstein over Crowley.

Social Darwinism assumes you have to fuck people over to survive

Social Einsteinism is natural selection nuanced by the gravity of a situation.

BALZAC'S 60 CUPS

They say Balzac drank 60 cups of coffee per day &
wrote 100 novels

Were the cups the size of thimbles?

Maybe it's true

I drink six cups a day &
wrote 10 books after all

The better part of mine
decaffeinated these days

One or two: the full ride
The gunpowder plot
That C-ticket

Banishing caffeine deficit disorder

I drink enough coffee to raise human-ness
to rise out of animal

Doubling down against adenosine
with a coffee nap
mid-afternoon

sleep when it comes
reorganizes enough sanity
thrown to disarray
by travail
to get me through another day

TOUCHING MADNESS

Heather, the all-nude stripper, coming out of Granny's Paradise Lounge on University warns us about this dude calling himself Madness who tried to pick up on her & fight her boyfriend. Angela & I go in the bar, order 2 pints of Foster's lager. As I'm browsing the jukebox, he sits next to her on the love seat. Returning with the pints, I sit in the middle. The guy must be drunk. He starts attacking my shoes, which aren't cool like his Doc Martens. Angela, always the appeaser, shows the guy pictures of our daughter & tells him about her. She tells this dude I'm Jimmy Jazz & asks if he's heard of me. No. He's a poet. I'm thinking I may have to fight. I feel scared. Can I finish my beer before I have to bash his slow skull with my pint glass? From his replies to Angela's questions, we glean that he works in the tool room at the shipyard & I notice a Minnesota accent. He's been to jail, twice, & had spent the day in court. Suddenly, the tough guy starts crying. Angela stands to offer a hug, believing her touch can heal. He needed to be touched. Either I hugged him or he hit you.

MARTIN LUTHER KING PARADE

Cecil & I were at the parade walking his dog, Drupes.

A boy of maybe five or six years kicked Drupes in the head, planting a tiny Chuck Taylor solidly under the dog's ear

So Cecil tracked the kid back to his mother

> Hey, your kid kicked my dog in the head.

> What do you want me to do? Hit him. It's just a dog.

Now Cecil loves his dog & I'm sure this lady loves her kid

> I want you to talk to him, that's what this day is about, the spirit of non-violence.

> This day is about me being here with my black brethren.

The story ends here & it's okay for readers, who are thinkers, to question Cecil's tone & unknown factors—like maybe Drupes was so scruffy it begged to be kicked

Nothing a Fire Can't Fix

X & Y

Murdered in 1965
as a horny white-suited sailor
impressed upon another short-skirted susie,
at shore leave, his seed

Riddled with bullets
as she with semen

> The crimson rush of blood
> sprayed his followers
> with the rich history
> of a bright continent, uncovered
> from the grim raper's cloud

His body toppled to the stage
as hers succumbed to hedonist desire
with a gangly thud

The cruel pop of flash-bulbs
illuminated the corpse for HEADLINES
in dire contrast to the dim yellow gaslamps
outlining the backseat groping forms
of two guilty creatures
sweating to escape the politics of the moment
without cause, without a cause
with anticipation of rumpled flesh & doting grandchildren
bouncing happily at couch-side safety

These are borrowed days of struggle

PAIN IS PAIN

Wallace Stevens
saying in a poem that Pain is Human

An esthetic disregarding meditations on the wind

Did you never see a dog miss the man?

Never saw a wolf in a steel trap gnaw loose a limb
Never saw an elephant lament
Never saw a stampede of burning deer leap from a forest on fire
Never saw a cow tremble before the slaughter ax
Never saw a dolphin cry

Nothing a Fire Can't Fix

SMALL POX

Let's say 100 people work on a farm picking cotton & along comes an invention, like say, the cotton gin, where 1 man can do the work of 100. I say that they should take turns, work 1 day & take 99 off. Since the same amount of cotton will come of it, they should collect the same wages as if they worked 100 days.

This happens all the time & we cede the profits to bosses & owners because in our hearts we are slaves.

Last week we got a new computer system that doubled my efficiency; shouldn't I work 4 hours instead of 8?

I'd call that progress.

A phone call currently costs fifty cents where it once costed a nickel; they call this "An advancement in technology." I call it thug-like thievery.

An advancement would mean that calls would cost a penny.[1]

Why is it that the newest & best cars pollute more than ever?
Why is it that I can't masturbate without a computer?
Why is it that politicians get paid & poets don't?

I'm sorry, but I have tried both; virtual sex is not an improvement.

Bombs are now so smart they hit the target 7 times out of 100.

Warfare has improved so much since caveman time that we had to invent the phrase "friendly fire."

Genetically engineered tomatoes are bigger & redder than ever, so what if they have no nutritional value unless crossed with a fish.

---

[1] In San Diego, you can still find a pay phone at your local library.

Corn that kills. Water with a list of ingredients on the side of the bottle. Diet Coke. Decaffeinated coffee. Fat free lard. Music without melody. Books without words. Life without death.

We've cured sadness & impotence & flatulence, but seven-hundred million people went to bed hungry & the girl who sewed your Nikes walked home barefoot from the factory.

You know something, shoes were more useful when they were made of wood

WALKING FUCK MACHINE

I'm a walking fuck machine
blind to her satisfaction buttons

Too focused on my dick, one supposes

Anthropomorphic // Narcissistic

suck fuck

You're upset, angry, I've noticed, how can I help?

Nothing, do nothing, just listen

But I'm a walking fuck machine

I can fuck your problems away

I can fuck problems under the rug, out the window, behind the fridge, I can fuck problems out to the garage with that thing your mom gave us for Xmas

I can fuck your problems away

ANTHROPIC PRINCIPLE

Who says language?
Who numbers?

A year works on earth

If you were born with four fingers,
you'd think eight was a magic number

Time is relative;
your cousins are always late

Light is a tear in the 5th dimension,
dripping down your cheek

Gravity is the most obvious &
weakest force in the universe

Nothing a Fire Can't Fix

SAINT TERSEA

Saint Tersea on the bed back
against the quilt warm
hair black flood along the pillow form
feet sewn to my pectoral fields

channel energy up up

naked paradise flush to the bed edge

me standing erect, she is thee farmer plowing her field

A man's palms firm spread across her hips holding
she just flapping that hoe flit flit in her garden

Oh, GyrAtion, I WANT IN, I'll trade my life,
the soles of my feet, my pen
let me stick it in when you cum let me stick it in

Oh Teresa

Lemme-

BAD RELIGION

I
I found this Bad Religion T-shirt in the pit at a rock show
Does it challenge or steel your faith?
Your symbol of love [oppression]
Your insignia of security [control]
Your peace sign is my octagonal red stop sign because what I value is different, not necessarily universally better, but different

And for me better

II
A concerned soccer dad walks up to me during the game

What is this Bad Religion?

The T-shirt sports the logo, a cross crossed out like a no parking sign & lists song titles like Fuck Armageddon This is Hell & Modern Man

> *Early man walked away & modern man took control, their minds were both the same, to conquer was their goal...*

The thing I like about Bad Religion, I say, is how they use four-syllable words

Oh no, says the concerned soccer dad. Lots of those rap groups use foul language

A second concerned soccer dad interjects, Not four-letter words, four-syllable words. SILL-LA-BULL

Early man walked away

Nothing a Fire Can't Fix

JESSE'S MOM BEATS HIM

Jesse's dad beats her
He's a little man, 5'1, he's a little man

Talks like he knows you

Jesse is a nasty boy showing his thing
to girls in the school's back closet

Saying suck it like he knows something
sweatier than lollipops

Jesse's mom beats him
Jesse's dad beats her

She's a big woman, 6'1, she's a big woman

Walking around like she don't know nothing

Jesse runs around the class
with his pants down, saying Fuck Fuck Fuck

Jesse's mom beats him
Jesse's dad beats her

BILE

You look like the kind of boy who would be popular in prison

You look like the kind of girl who meets Ted Bundy at the supermarket

You look like the kind of fat man who eats a half-gallon of ice cream in a sitting

You look like the kind of fat girl who doesn't want her uncle to touch her that way

You look like the kind of young woman who cultivates her zits as a rape shield

You look like the kind of old man who writes a check when the telemarketer screams

You look like the kind of slave that says, Yes sur boss

You look like the kind of cog who wastes his life in a factory

You look like the kind of coward who leaves 11 dead on a derailed train track after failing suicide

You look like the kind of teenage mother whose daughter will become a teenage mother

You look like the kind of 15-year-old Negro servant that a certain segregationist senator from South Carolina would knock up

You look like the kind of 12-year-old Lolita who tempts older gentlemen

You look like the kind of boy a priest would fondle

You look like the kind of groupie R. Kelly would pee on

Nothing a Fire Can't Fix

You look like the kind of drunk who sips discarded well drinks

You look like the kind of junkie who sucks dick in the public restroom

You look like the kind of smoker who dies of emphysema

You look like the kind of guy who did something amazing 10 years ago

You sound like the kind of immigrant who will never learn English

You sound like the kind of white liberal who doesn't confront crackers when they talk racist shit

You rap like the kind of rapper you heard on the radio

You look like the kind of debtor who buys a car at 26% interest

You look like the kind of slut who can't pick her baby daddy from a police line-up

You are the Viagra demographic

You are a poster child for keeping abortion safe & legal

You are the prom queen on the boulevard of broken dreams

You look like the kind of Xtian who tries to drive an SUV through the eye of a needle, the Muslim who straps a bomb to his chest, the Jew who drives a Mercedes, the atheist who says God bless you

You have the kind of face that men in wifebeaters like to slap

You have the kind of face that raises the dander on a border patrol agent's neck

You have the kind of face that cops slam into the hood

You have the kind of face that knows the difference between a quadratic equation & the square root of pi

You smell like the kind of bum who doesn't know which day the dumpster is emptied

You smell like the kind of hippie who thinks deodorant is a conspiracy

You think like the kind of woman who doesn't want to hear what's in the newspaper

You think like a soldier
You think like a thief
You think like a poet

BLADES OF GRASS

i write a curse word on a blade of grass—
a poet's anger in time of war

PESSIMIST

Angela said,
yesterday, I was a pessimist

I disagree

DIET

empty ocean
mad cow
bird flu
fat ass

I CANNOT LEAVE THIS HUMAN WORLD

Eyes closed

I'm conscious of the black before my eyes

I lose my eyes

I'm conscious of a pain in my hip

I lose my hip

I'm conscious of a far-off traffic din

I lose that traffic din

I'm conscious of the pressure on my landed ass

I lose my ass

I'm conscious of an itchy itch

I reach to scratch

Nothing a Fire Can't Fix

THE RHYTHM OF INERTIA

we are listening the radio
watching the television

instead of making the love &
talking our minds

we are like those neighbors we can't understand
so young, alive, unburdened by much

not fucking, not talking

watching the television

no money play dead no money

they don't, we don't
fuck or talk

watching the television
listening the radio

they don't, we don't

ELECTROWEAK THEORY

Just because Glashow unified
electromagnetism & the weak nuclear force

doesn't mean…
Ireland should wait for some new St Patrick
to reunite the island

Or that some two-bit messiah will
mitigate the woes of Israel & Palestine

Or the two Koreas
Or the North & the South
Or California v. everywhere

Then again, electromagnetism & nuclear decay
may also be superstitious human constructs
that seem to describe the world

Nothing a Fire Can't Fix

THE RUSE EVICTION

There will be no poetry

The ruse eviction The ruse eviction

'll break your bones & weave you through the wheel

The ruse eviction

'll hang you by the heels with a starved wolf

The ruse eviction

'll set the lumber saw between your legs- - - - - - - - - shh/shh

The ruse eviction

'll ease an electrified cucumber into your anus

The ruse eviction

'll run its tongue over your wounds & whisper in your ear

The ruse eviction

'll exile you to the desperate world

The ruse eviction The ruse eviction

> *Understand we're fighting a war we can't win //*
>
> *They hate us we hate them...*

In the morning, the sun rose upon a Poet
crucified by the lords of the land

In the morning, a poet's voice fell silent

In the morning, his tongue fell to ash

In the morning, el zopilote sailed the Santa Ana to a higher orbit
In the morning, the Actor starved
In the morning, Art sold out
In the morning, Music planned to sleep 'til noon
In the morning, Social Justice was nowhere to be found

In the morning, the commuters drove down Market—indifferent
In the morning, the iron heel of capital crushed a dream to rubble

In the morning, a hobo relieved himself in a vacant lot on the corner of 16th & Broadway

In the morning…trummerflora

In the morning, some meth head stole the Poet's shoes

In the morning, a drop of blood dripped onto the back of her filthy neck

Stupid pigeons roosting under the overpass

Nothing a Fire Can't Fix

STUPID DAYDREAMS

I have daydreams where I travel back in time to hang out with Thomas Jefferson

After a sumptuous meal at Monticello, he smokes a pipe of his pure tobacco & tells me about Burr's duel with Hamilton

On our midnight stroll back to the slave quarters
    I dislodge a brick, strike him, drop his pantaloons, & fuck him like a dog fucks another dog with barred teeth

My rocknroll band is more like Dillinger's gang holed up in a bank than The Stones at Petco Park - - - -Tommy gun guitars entice the audience, our hostages, to put their hands in the air (like they just don't care)

We're not a group so much as group sex

My time machine knocks holes in Columbus' boat,
slits Stalin's throat

Our hit song slinks:

I got a slow butt leak baby
on a Saturday night
my butt is itchin &
I'm raring to wipe…
I got a slow butt lēak

The lyrics aren't as lewd as the rhythm, which rolls out of Appalachia loaded like Tom Joad's truck

The jangle-bang bone cart of your body pushed through the years

Revising history only *seems* easier than making it

My stupid daydreams

My love for you

Blake touched a tree—remember trees—to pull himself into the material world

I'll touch anything:

A corpse on the streets of New Orleans
The key to a cage at Guantanamo bay
One of your pus-impacted piles

I'll do anything:

Wash the dishes
Talk to the weird neighbor who guards the garbage cans
Strike on May Day with the masses

The world is surreal, she says, like when we leave the house & our parents shed their clothes & chase each other through the kitchen with their walkers

WRITERS LIVERS

A writer writes
A liver lives, no
A liver filters poisons for the body
A writer filters poisons for the mind, no
A writer poisons minds stimulating unqualified joy & abject despair without regard for truth or necessity

Dostoevsky explained the necessity for despair

A WEDDING

My neighbors, Anne & Lance, decided to get married, which would have been illegal before WWII here in California when their grandparents were marrying people closer in skin tone

Anne sits across from her Filipina mother
Lance from his German mother

In celebration of a step

Studying the eerie mirror-like reflection, each wrinkle a mile, tension slowly relieved by the mutual will & want for grandchildren

AFTER A WEEK WITHOUT COFFEE, I DREAMT OF WILD HORSES

i'm running with a herd of wild horses
on the set of an old western movie
open expanse of sage & worried manzanita
oppressed by crows
through monument valley tetons aspiring in red chalk light

like all wild horses, a romantic

As equine fellows gather hungry weather-worn yet wild
i tell them of an orchard in a valley near the base of a cliff

> shuddering green leaves stabbed
> by bursts of brilliant red
> burnished bronze & spiral-floating-down like ripe fruit

the cool breeze of autumn braces courage
cantering from the herd to point the way
in a trot one, then another
soon we are running
we are wild horses & we are free
muscles undulate like amber waves of rocknroll
snap under glistening cosmopolitan coats
manes unfurling like black flags
we are running
we are wild horses & we are free

horses, horses, horses, horses

an orgy of speed
galloping, almost an eagle...

Now alone

The herd paused to masticate clover

Nothing a Fire Can't Fix

Lost, tensing as red eyes blink open like lit matches from the darkening gyre of rock

I can't go home to where my herd is, so head deeper into the canyon, walls steeply impassable, a slab of sheer granite present like a tombstone

Indignant panting stomachs snarl

A wolf stare analyzes you for weakness

Silence ferments

One with a puzzle piece torn from his left ear, says, "The wolves of wrath are wiser than the horses of instruction."

His attempt at humor fails to set me at ease

On the mesa, we see the herd, gait open to full stride, chased by a mastodon of dust

"Last words before supper?" one with gray fur asks

Wild horses couldn't drag me away

> I've grown thin & gamey, nearly knackered dry & tough with iron hooves & a solemn vow to crush one skull before I fall.

Wolves draw back their ears to show teeth

> Follow me to an orchard at the base of a cliff where we may all mute the wrath in our bellies with the still-warm flesh of fallen fruit.

In a dream, in a fable, all are fed. In life…

ALLEN GINSBERG

My dad called
        He read something about Allen Ginsberg &
besides his being gay, that guy is weird, has problems

Allen might agree

Making his problems public being Ginsberg's way of connecting
the scattered & shattered egos of humanity

He wants to access the transcendental diamond compassion & all
that, but dad says Ginsberg is not worthy of my esteem

The man is sick & should be shut away in an asylum, dad says,
unaware that he was, as his mother, as all the best minds

This is the way to peace, dad says,

    Lock up the criminals & perverts—the queers,
    activists & communists

Lock up the poets, I add, if they won't say what we tell them

Nothing a Fire Can't Fix

ROMAN MIDWINTER FESTIVAL TREE

Lies on the porch spent & browning
like a fallen soldier, slowly dying in the snow

bodyweight pulverizing a limb pinned
while maggots clean the wound

we soaked in its life, bathed in its life, oh so fragrantly

with merry cheer & the giving of gifts

needles needlessly swept away

THE SUN CALLED

The sun called through the open window

        Show me your cock

So I did

THE GOLD STANDARD

I wanted decency, for the tree. Ron Padgett

The story about Jesus whipping the money lenders
has invited me to compare the gold standard to the god standard

Karl & Abraham
Adam Smith & Joseph Smith
The Federal Reserve / The 700 Club
Reverend Rockefeller / Cardinal Ponzi

Your bible was written by a man
who looked like your father
who looks like your king
who looks like your god

A god that doesn't answer prayers
is like a stockbroker whose portfolio fails to perform
                Sometimes your stockbroker says, No.

The government used to say money had value
because backed by gold

Religious leaders used to say morality had value
because backed by miracles

We haven't seen any gold in Fort Knox for a long time

Capitalists & Xtians, when pressed, admit that both
monetary systems & religion are sustained by faith

As long as both parties believe that a 10-dollar paper bill
can be exchanged for a beer, you can quench your thirst

A financial crisis like a crisis of faith
devalues on the way to depression

Nothing a Fire Can't Fix

The old gods fell into recession with the last of their followers
No one believes Zeus sits on Mt. Olympus
or that Poseidon determines fate in the sea

Gas prices are on high

People like to point to written texts for moral authority

You could climb a Babel Tower of economic treatises,
like Faust out of Hell, & miss the black swan swooping out of the
darkening nimbostratus like a fire-breathing pterodactyl

The same people who used the bible to show an African was three-fifths man use the bible to claim a fetus is five-fifths human

To control a slave, dehumanize him
To control a woman, keep her pregnant

The Wall St Journal will not help you beat the stock market
better than a rabbit's foot in Vegas

The rich "demonize" the poor to keep them in their place

A story is a tool
A hammer pounds a nail
A story pounds customs, manners, values, law…
           Ask whose law

 In a sentence, it is best to be the subject

In the sentence:
  The priest rules over his subjects
       You are the object

A moral system isn't good because somebody wrote it down
Times a-changin', values e-volvin'

Moses, that hypocrite, stole the ten commandments

from the Hittites, after all

    Thou shalt have no other gods before me, said the god

    Six days shalt thou labour, said the slaveholder

    Honor thy father & thy mother, said thy PARENTS

    Thou shalt not kill, unless you're the king said thy king

    Thou shalt not commit adultery, said thy wife

    Thou shalt not steal, said thy landlord

    Thou shalt not covet thy neighbor's ass—well...
        whoever said this hasn't seen my neighbor's ass

I'm not saying live without rules
only that if we want to live around people
we need no authority
but ourselves

to hash out & rehash a morality

- your freedom ends where mine begins
- our equality can be sustained by mutual aid
- we must protect the environment for all creatures

sentient, insane, illiterate or indifferent, which is, again,
the bottom line

Nothing a Fire Can't Fix

SLINGSHOT

The tide a giant slingshot
loaded with a pale marble
to put out the sun

THE OBSERVABLE UNIVERSE

The Earth is at the center of the observable universe,
if that makes you feel better

An eyelash in a flash flood is man
Less than a blink in a light year
A planetesimal teardrop in The Oort Cloud

You are almost nothing

You are nothing

You are gone

MY AUNT, MY MOTHER'S SISTER

I spend too much money & too much time in dive bars in dive hoods drinking dive beer with dive people.

Tonight: It's City Heights

No trees, barking dogs bang the gate. The place where smog goes to die on dirty asphalt. The houses are shacks with plywood shades, the local market a gas station, the dropout hangout will cash your check, graffitied walls shout malcontent, the corner store sells malt liquor in half-gallon cartons with the forlorn faces of forgotten children wielding the memory of smiles like a rusted blade...

Stairway to Charo is playing. They cover old Zeppelin & Sabbath tunes with Charo as the singer. Carmen Miranda as Ozzie Osborn shaking her maracas. Hoochie Coochie.

> *Come cruise with me in my Impala // And we'll go to Varrio Logan*

I was up front banging my head, jumping around screeching: Ay ay ay ay ay!

I looked back at the crowd, saw mostly 20-something minor hipsters, like myself, digging the parody. The old gray bartenders were getting a kick out of it too because the original tunes came from their generation. Then this raggedy couple of too-beat junkies walked in. The man's face was covered by a grizzly vermin-infested beard, his eyes were smoky & dirty like his clothes. The exposed skin of his face was like a rotten piece of meat burnt & scabbed over by the sun.

The woman was even more beat. Her kicked around pigskin face looked like an old brown lunch sack carried to school & back. She was a Popeye Seahag with tangled weedy blonde hair, her liver rotted by too much drink & too much speed, altering the skin tone

Nothing a Fire Can't Fix

to an inhuman orange-brown—like an Oompa Loompa.

She looked like one of those speed hags who sucked shitty sweaty open sore gonorrhea cocks for meth or money. Like she'd been sleeping in lice mattress flops, begging change on Eleventh Avenue…I was surprised. Stunned, speechless, I couldn't talk, I couldn't talk to her, I never can:

She's my aunt, my mother's sister.

She gave me Hot Wheels for Xmas 1973, my mom said she probably ripped them off from Toys "R" Us, working the holiday rush, but mom was angry because of the grief she gave their mom, my Nana. My aunt, my mother's sister was always stealing money out of Nana's purse for drugs or food. On Nana's Lucky Strike death bed, my aunt, my mother's sister ripped off her pain medication… probably to support a loser boyfriend, like the one who'd taken too many pills with booze, passed out two days with his leg bent back funny, too stoned to roll over, the leg turned green & died, they had to cut the whole thing off. He played flute in the park, Bill was his name. I liked him when I was a kid, thought he was cool, thought my aunt, my mother's sister was cool too.

My aunt, my mother's sister begs change on Eleventh Avenue, spending your coin on smack or crack in nose in arm eat it smoke it stuff it in your ass.

Remember the War against Drugs?

The United States vs. My Aunt, My Mother's Sister.

Local paper: "Joan Kroc GIVES $100 to poor Homeless woman and child on 11th Avenue."

Before my uncle, my mother's brother rescued him, my cousin was on the street for three years. Blonde hair like his mama, blue eyes like me. A couple toys on the downtown sidewalk. Kid was bug-lousy & whacked out when they got him. Telling stories about strange penises, naked movies, naked parties, naked naked

naked…

Can you see what's on the end of the fork?

I used to see my cousin every time I went downtown to check out bands like Royal Crown Review at Bodie's.

Let's juxtapose my aunt, my mother's sister to the made-up-before-the-mirror rockabilly swing dance dolls:

They both get their clothes at thrift stores.
They both get wasted on Saturday night.
They both get down for money, one way or another.

Don't we all?

I should've given money, given food, got my family off the street, but I did nothing.

I was afraid.

I was afraid they'd ask to crash at my pad, that I'd wake up robbed.

I had my own problems.

Don't we all?

She's standing across the bar. I could make things right, I could try. She stumbled in off the street. This joint's on the bus route. Maybe her crash pad crack house flop is nearby.

It's a shooting gallery world & we're all sitting ducks.

She stumbled back in time. Kevin "pied piper" Chanel on guitar.

She probably thinks this is a cover band, of her old favorites. She saw Zeppelin & Sabbath in their straight-up hippie heyday.

Summer of '68 alright.

Nothing a Fire Can't Fix

My aunt, my mother's sister has the biggest smile on her face.
She's playing air drums, really into it. Banging & shaking & smiling.
She's somewhere back in time with her pretty face & blonde hair
bouncing in the sun just washed.

So young so innocent.
She's back in high school.

Saturday Night is for kicks & thrills.

She's tossing her hair to the music.

Grinning, really digging it.

Her teeth don't look too bad.

She walked out.

The band was still playing, I was still trying to gather enough
courage to talk with her.

SATURDAY MORNING WHITTLES AWAY

I cannot move

So much to do
bizzy like dizzy
tune up the car
smog check the car
pay the ticket before it doubles
pay the registration
vacuum the car
clean the car
the car the car
the car

walk

WEIRDO

You're weirdo, she says

After stealing my spot on the couch &
taking a bite from a saltine cracker,

she picks her teeth with a pinky nail

Nothing a Fire Can't Fix

FILM STUDENTS

I spotted you three blocks away
Neo-platinum wig screaming

You can't have this Penis Boys,
I've French kissed a woman

CECIL

CECIL KEEPS CALLING WANTS TO DRINK &

PLAY PINBALL... I'M STUCK

WITHOUT A PULSE, NO WILL, BUT TO SIT

PARADIGM SHIFT

I'm on the edge of a paradigm shift
I may crack at work
I may strangle a pet
I may curl up in a naked ball & die

I WANNA BE YOUR ROACH

Opaque black bugs
Legions
Tumors
Composters

Beautiful rodilating composters triumphal

Give America's refuse back to the earth
Outlive Humanity a thousand decades
Digest the phony plastic world

Crawl

I'll be your pet, your puppet radio
Keep me on a leash, tell me what to say

We fear you   Crawl over the sleeping faces
Polish the bones of the dead
Stand the living on chairs

Make them squeal

Squeal

Cross a path like a black cat
Make them dance
Teach them to live

You terror, you electric shock

Fear not the boot

Madness is your consequence
Out from behind the walls
Eat Reproduce Crawl
            over the sleeping faces of a dead world

Nothing a Fire Can't Fix

HISTORY IN THE DOCUMENT SHREDDER

What would you do if <u>your</u> brother was the Unabomber?

What would you do if you witnessed a rape?

•••

What would you do if your uncle trained killers, overthrew elected governments, sold drugs to the ghetto, funded death squads, & bombed defenseless peasants?

Oliver North put Iran & Nicaragua
in the document shredder together

Ignore Ignore // I told you before
acquiescence means "nothing" to me

Henry Kissinger shredded Cambodia
  over cocktails with Nixon

In Haiti, the CIA trained Death Squads to kill thousands
  the records were shredded in nineteen-ninety-four

In Guatemala, we assassinated Mayans
  for the United Fruit banana corporation
  the details were shredded to prevent prosecution
  we invaded in fifty-four

Ignore ignore El Salvador
  where the right-wing Death Squad torture of tu abuelito
  was funded by taxes on American dildos
  in the Washington DC suburbs

Freedom of Information is a misnomer
Someone must <u>pay</u> attention

We may never know who loaned Iraq money to buy weapons
during the CNN Gulf War miniseries,
   since the Department of Agribusiness shredded the evidence
   in the Wholesale-destruction-of-justice Department

Cuba & Italy, Angola & Spain,
Panama, Tibet, & The Philippines,
Grenada, Indonesia, Vietnam, & Korea

While rights to the oil under Native treaty lands
were "lost" which means shredded
somebody got rich

When a politician says "National Interest,"
he means business

In Columbia, we're supporting a military dictator
   listen while the media prepares you for war
   (there's kidnapping & cocaine lords & resources like coffee)

Back home the economy is stronger than ever before
So give the Unabomber a room in the mansion with Noriega &
leave the slave owning-rapist on Rushmore

Nothing a Fire Can't Fix

IS 74 OLD ENOUGH?

I live a dainty life of healthy intake
fat free   sodium free   Or-r-r-r-ganic
I don't smoke
I drink in moderation
to temper the heart
I sleep regular hours
I should exercise more & resolve to do so,
while Bukowski drank enough licker
to still any man's heart & piss the Yangtse

With luck, I'll live to be 80 or 90

Sixteen more years than Hank to eat pussy &
whack off to classical music

If I'm not blind, think of the books I'll read
If I'm not deaf, think of the music I'll hear
If I'm not too arthritic, think of the poems I'll write
If I haven't sold my soul to god, think of the fun I'll have

THE UNTRIED STATES OF POETRY

When Kenneth Starr held the Blue Dress to the light,
in the stain he saw the image of the Virgin of Guadeloupe

Ask yourself why you do it & refuse to breathe until you
manufacture consent

Look in the mirror; deny the misanthropy etched in your pores

Name your blackheads after Greek myths

I wish they would build the sink closer to the toilet,
so that I could piss & wash my hands at the same time

Fly under the poverty line, like a missile under the radar

Join a union for people who don't want to work

Where the naked lunch wrecking ball new wine unheard music
pirate enclave?

Where the babel tower starship submarine X-ray?

Where the Stonewall Haymarket dinner party jihad & witch trial
crucifixion?

Maybe there are too many poets

We regionalize, anthologize,
separate into camps, choose schools,
more like kickball teams than armies,
we disperse

Nothing a Fire Can't Fix
MINIMALIST MUSEUM

Blank Canvas
Acrylic on canvas

Poems

White on White
Acrylic on canvas

Translucent Black
Acrylic on canvas

Nothing a Fire Can't Fix

Nothing is Real
Acrylic on canvas

Everything is Permitted
Acrylic on canvas

Malevich
Acrylic on canvas

Martin
Acrylic on canvas

Rauschenberg
Acrylic on canvas

Nothing a Fire Can't Fix

Protest
Mixed Media

Poems

Untitled #23
Acrylic on canvas

Nothing a Fire Can't Fix

White Girl (living in a white world)
Acrylic on canvas

White Boy Shuffle
Acrylic on canvas

Poems

Tabula Rasa
Acrylic on canvas

Nothing a Fire Can't Fix

Wells
Acrylic on canvas

Ellison
Acrylic on canvas

Poems

Cloud in (white duck) Trousers
Acrylic on canvas

A Fly in the Milk, drowned
Acrylic on canvas

Sunbleached Skull, high noon
Acrvlic on canvas

A Polar Bear, asleep on its paws
Acrylic on canvas

wonderbread
Acrylic on canvas

gated community
Acrylic on canvas

vanilla sex
Acrylic on canvas

Absence
Acrylic on canvas

Loss
Acrylic on canvas

Poems

Unlimited Potential
Acrylic on canvas

Unfinished Work
Acrylic on canvas

Nothing a Fire Can't Fix

Posthumous
Acrylic on canvas

EVENT HORIZON

We were supposed to meet at this event that his work sponsored on a Saturday, but when we got there his friends & co-workers pulled him in he... disappeared... leaving me standing by the no-host bar with a lo-ball of Johnnie neat & an open credit card bearing his name

BLACK HOLE

black hole
   a mirror
catching images with light held close

Children on carousels
Modern man clubbing Neanderthal

STRANGE ATTRACTOR

Trying to figure out why I like you,
little butterfly,
but it doesn't add up

My dad is a painter
we'd meet by the ocean
look at art, eat some lunch

MEMORY PALACE

ghost dark college campus
using my Sub novel
teaching how not to teach

unruly poet slam
$500 bucks at stake
Boyce reads with O_2 tank

the restless teenagers
park nights on Soledad
learning sex in their cars

the restless teenagers
wander around the night
looking for some trouble

Klam catches a big wave
dropping from the peak, gone
a black dolphin swims by

a stolen bicycle
chase carload of gangsters
a cop said, "That was dumb."

after thirteen long hours
nurse appears with baby
hands her to grandpa first

Giant Dipper coaster
I'm two inches too short
wait 13 years to ride

a secret film noir night
cottage above the sea
a pint, "For all my friends."

tourists pay too much dough
for less Mmmm burritos
the mariachi tax

Stiff Little Fingers play
a small club, Jake Burns growls
Bruce Foxton on bass

Pride parade in Hillcrest
Ashley, who is seven,
asks us, "Is that dog gay?"

the tall buildings downtown
like men behind closed doors
lost in the morning fog

selfie with Pancho Villa
rather live on my feet
a park under the bridge

walk down 3rd with Nana
Eiger Sanction at The Vogue
I am but nine years old

pricey border fence, mom
passes conchas through bars
keep them out, keep us in

modicum of danger
for young Americans
drug cartels kill fodder

May Gray/June Gloom abides
September summer
don't tell the damn tourists

mer Padre pitcher
ns the local carwash
spotless hall of fame

boys by the old lake side
fear a sheep molester
called Chester, serious

-ache, walking backwards
ill to the car post game
did we park way up here?

hike out to the old mine
shaft sign: HANTAVIRUS
in line for apple pie

ocotillo sprouts like
a squid, tentacles ro-
dilate in the hot wind

12 green parrots squawking
in the mountain ash tree
eat dumb rowanberries

a lunatic screaming
"dirty pedophile fuck"
hurling baseballs rebound

HOW REFRESHING

We killed those guys because we wanted their stuff

We raped those women so our enemies would have better genes

We mutilated clits so not to waste time rubbing them

We fucked little boys because tiny buttholes make us feel big

We moved their houses because the minerals thereunder help us live comfortably

We started this war to keep them from getting organized

We launched that cruise missile to refocus public opinion

We made slaves of children so ours could eat chocolate Easter bunnies

We flooded their valley because they aren't really human & because we like waterskiing

We bombed that clinic because there aren't enough poor people to push around

We got six wives because we like sex six times more than first wife

We stoned those sinners to keep sin exciting (& edgy)

We invented TV, so Gilligan's Island could become immortal

We made up that deity, so we could collect tithe—aka taxation without representation

We bought an SUV because global warming is submerging Bangladesh too slowly

We sent that boy to the chair because instilling fear is a good way to consolidate power

We slaughtered our neighbors before they could slaughter us

We built that fence because we thought it would be funny to see Mexicans crawl through tunnels to bring us drugs

We ignore science because it's hard to understand
We ignore facts because they don't say what we want
We ignore poets because they won't say what we tell them

Nothing a Fire Can't Fix

A LITTLE BRAINLESS CHILD

I look back to see how I got here,

        a brainless child throwing a tennis ball

against the stucco house
for hours

OBLIVION

I blow a pubic hair off the table
Does it really disappear?

or

A child flicks a good booger from her finger
Does it land nowhere?

LIFE SAVERS

Hart Crane's father
a candy magnate
invented the Life Saver

EDUCATIONAL EXPERIENCE

My cousin came to spend a few days with us.
He's 17 & a half. (The half!)

We saw Pulp Fiction.
Made an Art film with Lulu Godardo.
We walked downtown.

A man asked my cousin for fifty cents.

He reached in his pocket,
looked at the quarter which came to hand, &
gave it to the man.

Who, in turn, gave my cousin a Kiss-o-Mint condom.

It's probably expired, I told him.

Don't strap that on your dick to fuck.

Nothing a Fire Can't Fix

EMPLOYEE OF THE MONTH

A boss's tool
to sew dissent
a division of labor————-ers

He chooses the shirker
to piss everyone off

Bowie refused knighthood
Sartre rejected a Nobel

Next time, divide
whatever crumb
they toss
with the team
at the meeting
to plot

a fair wage

I AM A MORON

I am a moron
a dolt
of little intellect
my perception is limited
my intuition is indigent
like a bum I travel through this world
begging warmth & food & love
I have no capacity for survival
no instinct of worth

A talentless buffoon
substituting competence with mild chicanery
a dragoon of the lowest order
following in the ranks of mindless minions
I will obey the laws & work to conform the children of god into
calm, happy wage slaves

My loves are petty, the heights I'll attain ridiculous in their
minuteness

The temper of a good dog

    KILL ME

Nothing a Fire Can't Fix

COFFEE SHOP HIP HOP

Nothing like the feeling of

Getting work done rag

Getting organized boogie-woogie

Success honky tonk

Completed task & product opera

>Sing hallelujah
>Sing glory

Blesséd mother goddess of work ethic

Sing to me praise I-nan-na

Ginsberg has his father death blues &
I have this coffee shop hip hop
People fly him in to read poems
I've never been on a plane &
people fly from the scene of my poems

>Screaming No-o-o-o-o-o-o-o

THEY SAY

Drink 8 glasses of water a day
Drink two glasses of wine
Drink 6 cups of coffee

Eat Quinoa, Acai, Chia
Use sunscreen
Meditate
Take 10,000 steps
Take 8,000

Have more sex
Have less sex
Use a condom

Floss

Take vitamins
Don't take vitamins
Take zinc supplements

They say stress is bad
They say do crossword puzzles

Get married
Don't get married
Get a dog

They say listen to your elders
Do the right thing
Don't sit so close to the TV

Put your food on a plate
Don't eat in a car
Water your friends

Nothing a Fire Can't Fix

THE PIG RITUAL

The neighbors have a pig
Big & heavy in its lifelessness

A single bright incandescent bulb illuminates the scene
Ranchera music rings from their open kitchen door

The men, three men, have an excited tension
galvanizing their bodies with spiritual energy

The electricity runs out of gestures in & around the scene
One man—the Pig Expert—shaves the pig's hair or skin with a razor, a manner of expertise, watched his father cooking pigs in old Mexico

The village is festive

A child, a girl, looks on, eating candy
The men drink Budweiser from cans—

Could I join them?
Should I pick up a case of Tecate at the corner store?
Could I join?

Angela says,
    We can't eat that pig
    We don't eat pigs
    We don't harm animals
    We're vegan

                                                 off the pigs fuck the pigs

Even if I wanted to eat their pig
TRUTH reveals a lack of social skills or real will to transcend the language, culture, & class barriers

I'm afraid... I have a problem with authority... I'm afraid...

I'm afraid of the pig ritual

The Pig Ritual, the pig ritual...

Their PIG is so BIG
                    It's dead

Through death, night & community come to life—a flourish this neighborhood hasn't seen since the fisherman were lost at sea

      Imagine the holiday fish fry

The drunken laughter
the voices in Portuguese, Italian & English, in Spanish

The Pig Ritual
The Pig Ritual
The Pig Ritual

You see what you eat, in seeing what you eat you see what you are

The pagan ritual: kill it, cook it, carve it

The pig, the pig ritual

                                          off the pigs
You feel what you eat, consumer become the hunter
connoisseur trim the fat, voyeur gut the innards

The ritual, the pig ritual

They have her legs spread & her teats shed
That pig is ready to cook

                                          fuck the pigs

El Gordo lying on his side
  an old ranch hand struck a pig with a club
El Gordo roasting in a pit
turning on a spit
burning in his skin

Nothing a Fire Can't Fix

We won't go hungry for a few days
        Our friends our families

    Hamon
        Adobada
                Pork Pork Pork
Hamon
        Adobada
                Pork Pork Pork

Chorizo spices ready
                            Posole by Sunday

La Gorda lying on her back
for a good porking
shave her teats with a razor
Hold her arms   Hold her legs
La Gorda on her back
        I'm gonna eat her
gonna lick my lips   gonna lick the fingers
that tear into her meaty pig flesh
La Gorda lying on her back

THE PHILATELIST

licks a rare stamp
with the deft facility &
deep reverence
of the Bonobo
gleaning the asshole
of his copulate

THREADBARE

Tamara pointed out my threadbare socks
Saying nothing about the filthy robe
The hole in my slippers
My graying, balding hair
The weakening muscles nor
The forget-filled mind

POVERTY

Poverty weighs-in heavy
before his big fight with the champ

Not just the cost of things
but the true cost of things

CONSENSUAL SEX AMONG THE TURTLES

[bomp bomp bomp bomp]

I started fucking you
in the most southwesterly
corner of the dusty pen

A horny zoo turtle

[bomp bomp bomp bomp]

I looked up to see who was knocking &
realized your head was banging on
the northernmost wall

TURTLE

I saw turtle alive
        He had eyes
but the eyes were flies

ANTHROPOTACTIQUE

My daughter's dog has separation anxiety

Who's a good boy?

Do you fear everything good will be snatched away
each time she leaves for work?

Does hope rise & fall like the heavy breath inside your chest?

What does your sigh mean?

Will you disengage in her absence from things you seem to love:

Sniffing where other dogs have walked

Barking at the mail carrier, that enemy who won't cross the threshold

Bounding out the door to catch the cat

Scarfing food, begging food

If you—dog—refused to eat,
I'd say dogs were human

EINSTEIN-ROSEN BRIDGE

    My thoughts are so massive
  that space-
time
warps
  around me

come close &
                       you'll orbit

like flakes of skin & hair circle a drain

rodilating

the earth, the sun
the sun, the galaxy

a halo of flies

Some people say a black hole
is a bridge to another universe

RACIST BOMB THREAT

At the Washington School (92% Hispanic) where my daughter
attends first grade, someone called in a bomb threat

A copycat selling fear to ••••, V, six & 11 of the clock news
|||||||||||||||||||||||| ||||||

The Federal Building horror in Oklahoma cracked the nation with
spidery tendrils erupting from the glassy epicenter out to the
collective conscience where public opinion lives

And all they could come up with was:

THE RACE WAR IS COMING

Not the class war we expected, but the ugly Xtian white god party
asserting its privilege

The racists say the Mexicans are after "our" jobs, as if the Mexicans
weren't fellow humans seeking sustenance

Our jobs? Ha. You don't even like your job

Threatening to kill children
frightening my child, a little girl

To forward what cause but hate?

A poem, like those gruesome images, can't stop crazy

KILLING TIME

Art is a time-killing machine
Voyeurism is a time-killing machine
Meditation is not the same as sitting around with nothing to do
Sex doesn't last long enough to be a time-killing machine
Poets are not comedians
When we pander, we stop being poets
One should not attempt a time-killing machine until a certain level of safety, food, shelter, & love is

The socialists want to everyone attain a time-killing machine

A capitalist on Madison Avenue thinks he has a clever marketing strategy for a time-killing machine

What a strange creature is time
dead on a slab
with 365 bones
12 major organs
24 eyes & 60 pints of blood

The dead seconds fall by the wayside
History is the biggest slaughter in history

FREE LUNCH

Lydia Lunch invited me to read from my work in Los Angeles, so I drove from San Diego, not so far really. She made a flyer on color card stock, listed calendar items in all the papers.

No one came to the reading, not one person, so I called Lydia.

>"Oh, I'm in Paris."

The bartender said, "Drink whatever you want on us."

JACK HIRSCHMAN, JACK MARSHALL, JACK SPICER

battered cardboard box donated
to the Friends of the Library
an old beat poet musta died

Did I buy all 30 books for 30 bucks?

Did Kerouac steal the wine from that party uptown?

Nothing a Fire Can't Fix

STOLEN CAR

Woke
up angry
snapped at the little girl
clenched teeth (like my father's)
Let every letdown
stir my stew
Punched an empty box
Socked & knocked the magnets off the refrigerator
GOD DAMN
GOD DAMN
GOD DAMN
Wanting to see our stolen car so I could pulp the thief
with The Club
bashingskulltomushbloody
tortturepoundingonlifelessflesh
frustrationfists
poundingkillkillkill

THE CLUB

Hank Thoreau kept an extra chair & cup at Walden Pond; Ted Kaczynski didn't.

Friends ask hard questions.

Michael Klam: Why do you lock The Club to your car steering wheel?
    Because my car had been stolen three times.

I thought about it all through breakfast. I thought about Michael Moore asking why Americans lock their doors while Canadians don't. I thought about William Upski Wimsatt claiming to walk through America's 20 worst ghettos at midnight.

Am I contributing to the culture of fear?

My grandmother looks through her electronic window & sees the gurgling maw of apocalypse.

What if some desperate person needed my car to escape?
I don't need a blaring alarm to protect my car.
I don't need a car; I can walk.

I can walk through the ghetto at midnight.

Tamara Johnson: Did you hear about the angry motorist on the freeway battering a second angry motorist with The Club?

I thought about it over lunch. I thought about John Zerzan, when asked how much society we should abandon, saying, "How free do you wanna be?"

Am I contributing to the culture of fear?

My father looks through his front windshield and sees traffic.
Moved from California to Iowa to avoid it.

Nothing a Fire Can't Fix

A story on the news reminded me of Pierre Proudhon saying, "Property is Theft"

In Amsterdam, they held yellow bicycles in common. In Portland, someone stole the yellow bicycles, painted them black, & sold them at garage sales.

I don't need a club, a gun, or an army to protect my national interests. I don't need any weapons; I have no national interests.

At midnight, don't graffiti on fences, remove them.

Cecil Hayduke: Do you wanna sit on the blue Naugahyde couch we found by a dumpster & shoot other discarded objects with a slingshot?
      Fuck yeah.

I thought about it the next day at work, like Cecil walking away from the job & the money in pursuit of something unknown & uncertain.

Am I contributing to the culture of fear?

My mother thinks the news is a spectacle to entertain her.

After the repo man took Cecil's Mercedes, he quit dating strippers & buying pints for the bar. He got a bike.

I don't need to waste my life as a slave to meaningless work. I don't need to work. I quit my job every time I read this poem.

When you've got nothing, you've got nothing to steal.

One blue Naugahyde couch, three extra cups, & a bottle of wine is all we need.

BRUISES OF MOOD (BLACK BLUES)

a black widow
a black hole
a black heart
a black night
her black skin
black gold
  a black plague
  a black day
some black coffee
a black sky
your black clothes
the black blues
a black man
a black woman
a black child
a black bird

ITERATIONS

Friends form a world
utterances of the moment momentously impact
      ricocheting off the known

                                        to make

Resonating through

All the best lines from books
      stored in some combination of cells

Riffing movie quotes like
           "Plate of Shrimp"

Chunks of song writing & re-writing themselves

The morass of input   competing to stick

Things your mom told you
      Things you heard on the street

Being an outsider, distrusting inside jokes
      Cecil knew about Glue
           mocking awkward attempts to include

Before a gig Klam used to say, Let's teach.
And Cecil, Fuck Shit Up.
SeyMour would say, Look! Look! Look!
And Shinya once said, Doi-oi-oi-oi-oing!

Yet Angela has to say, Live in the moment,
over & over & over

Tamara Johnson showed, without saying a word,
      The greatest poem was a beard

SHORT LINES

I asked my students
to write poems
saying it was easy:

Take that chair:

>A black chair
>with silver arm rests
>in the corner

And the Swiss girl said
That's not a poem

>Maybe a poem is an image

But a good poem reaches for the reader
with humor or something to think about
or a feeling

And the Saudi guy said
That's not a poem, it's a thought

>Maybe a poem is a thought

into to short lines
broken

RIEMANNIAN GEOMETRY

When Einstein couldn't make Euclid work
for General Relativity,
he called on a different geometry…

When standard numbers fail to describe the world,
a physicist invents new ones…

So devise anew
    communication
    sex
    ways of not killing

SCHRÖDINGER'S CAT

Does a tree make a sound if no one hears?

Who cares?

Is Schrödinger's cat dead or alive?

Pandora balks
Hawking reaches for his gun

Schrödinger has died

cover the box
with earth

WHERE LIFE IS INAPPROPRIATE

We withhold powerful realities

The abortion you had last week more real & now & affective than
the American Revolution in our textbook // more powerful than
bull shit promises made by the Bill of Rights

The kids can't
        You can't
                I don't
dare (if I wanna keep this job)
push the limits of free speech in the workplace because

at school

Life is Inappropriate

RUNNING FOR CHOMSKY

What are you running for?
What are you running for?

                                        CHOMSKY

He's been talking shit since 1955 & one day he's gonna die

So we better be ready with a new   CHOMSKY

Ready to question every assumption
Ready to criticize media diversion
Ready to call hypocrisy a liar to his face

We need a new Chomsky

The office of Chomsky shouldn't be confused with
the Ministry of Conspiracy or Crackpot General

We need someone to write
how the left ain't left enough
for the poor to eat
How money frames the debate
How slavery is manufactured by cajoled consent

We need a living wage
We need government that doesn't support iron-handed dictators
for the bottom line
We need intellectuals
       who are NOT afraid
       who will NOT kiss the ass of private power
       who are NOT benevolent princes to watch over us
       who WILL read between the lines
       who have the WILL to read between the lines

We need a new Chomsky
We need a thousand chomskys

And an analysis of & owning

    OUR HISTORY

(Columbus was a slave-trading rapist... systematic slaughter of the Indians... land stolen from Mexico... Jim Crow... we plotted we plotted we plotted to assassinate Lumumba with poison toothpaste... McDonald's beef tallow french fry lies... I'm sick sick sick sick of their lies)

He's been talking shit since 1955 & one day he's gonna die

I'm not saying we need a pretty chomsky to put on TV
we need a fat chomsky
we need a black chomsky
we need women & children chomskys &
a faggot chomsky too

I'm a low-ridin zoot-suit jivin ganja smoking Oscar Zeta Acosta bomb throwin chomsky

I'm a garbage man chomsky & I not only vote, I run for office

forming forming forming

grassroots coalitions with
red, white, blue, & yellow chomskys
to put into practice what we preach
liberty & justice for <u>ALL</u>

Not for some   FOR ALL
Not for some   FOR ALL

Nothing a Fire Can't Fix

WATCHED THE LIFE & TIMES OF ALLEN GINSBERG

Reminded me, as I rail against stupidity [what cynics do] that the Middle Class, that apathetic beast, is not my enemy

Nietzsche reminded me that Pity is not a panacea, not even a flea collar savior from the starving rabid animal bony finger o' death claws of that bitch called money

The Middle Class is my docile puppy dog grown
old with skin disease

Dry hairless patches flake where a naïve boon to play panted & drooled in happy lateral locomotion, commotion, & hype

My Middle Class is no sled dog pulling supplies to the frontier

Where politicians be lapdogs of the rich

My Middle Class is a Goldfish
belly-up & bloated with water log diversions

My poor stupid silly Middle Class
I'll laugh at your wake

You lazy cur Middle Class
What will happen to your values?
Your ambition to be fed?

You scarfed a planet & left nothing for your children
The poor peasantry of hanging out to dry rags for clothes

DOGS DOGS

Little runty nervous pissing dogs

DOGS DOGS

The Middle Class Dog The Middle Class Dog The Middle Class Dog The Middle Class Dog The Middle Class Dog The Middle Class Dog The Middle Class Dog The Middle Class Dog

    Middle/middling/mediocre/median/mild

Dog Dog Dog

Old sad stupid puppy, go bury your old bones

Nothing a Fire Can't Fix

YOU ARE YOUR RIGHT HAND

About to fight at school, my hand would shake

Forced to speak in front of class, I would stutter, even lose my voice

There have been times, like hitting 30, when the *blood wouldn't come when it ought to come*

Last night my right hand stepped out to kill

My protesting heart was dismissed as a special interest group
Forty-seven percent of my brain said Kill or be killed, with us or against us, don't be a coward, this body is the best body, their brains are bad brains, their thoughts, if thoughts, are evil thoughts

Fifty-three percent didn't vote

The rest of my body did nothing
My left leg stood there
My pancreas was silent
My ears shut their eyes & covered their mouths

My aorta waved a flag

Who was my right hand taking orders from:

The stomach?
The dick?
The asshole?

The cow is not her milk; the hat don't make the man, but you are your own right hand

DOREMEQUISHA

On the phone with your guardian
manic in the moment yelling,

Do-re-me-quisha get down here. What you been doing in your class?

  Talking while others talk
  Talking while teacher gives directions
  Singing, she's always singing

Singing? She know better, I raised my children & she ain't special

I come down to that school, you turn your head, & I'll slap her damn mouth

Doremequisha got 21 people in jail
She the last one
Her mom in jail, her brother got 25 yrs
Her cousin, my son, got 25 to life
Her whole family on dope

> A set of hep-yellow brown eyes, no whites, no pupils, hold six white teachers in check

Don't look at me with those eyes teacher man
> He averts his eyes

I'm going for surgery on the 7th, the cancer, tumors
Doremequisha never had anyone she could love

> We feel guilty for her behavior

I know she's a bitch, her guardian says, she gets that from her mother

We'll be homeless, if I live

Nothing a Fire Can't Fix

1937

Johnny Johnson hopped out of a boxcar in Cedar Falls, Iowa, where one of his brothers had a job

His oldest sister became a missionary in China
His youngest, a showgirl in Vegas
Six Johnson boys served on ships
around the Pacific in the war

He'd hitched from LA headed for Boston to visit cousins he'd never seen & touch the dock where his father jumped ship from Sweden to become American

As luck would have it, Mommer & Papa had driven out to fetch his brother home

> *Johnny what are you doing here?*
> *Going to Boston ma*
> *Have you got any money, son?*
> *Yes sir pop*, he fibbed

His father handed him a crackling' five-dollar bill
like 100 bucks back then

Roosevelt was president
Hitler was on the march
Japan had invaded China

Johnny caught a ride into Detroit, driver looked straight ahead but reached to feel his thigh

"I jumped out of that car so fast," he'd say telling the story

Roll, shake dust, & walk on

His cousins called him "Hollywood" &
he taught them to do the Balboa like they did in Newport

Shaw, Ellington, Basie, Miller, & Prima were the big bands

My grandma's dad called him "Slats" joking if he turned sideways he'd disappear, but he was persistent, even cocky, with his hair slicked, as sharp as his suit

"We were dancing fools," she used to say

He laughed, danced, made a baby, went to war, bowled with the Elks, waterskied to Catalina, played golf, followed baseball, shot pool, drank Johnnie Walker; he got two grand & two great-grand kids

He worked his whole life

Until lymphoma laid him down at 80
listening to gospel music with one arm aloft

Visiting grandma, as she prepared for her own death, I caught her taking photos out of her albums & dropping them in a black plastic trash bag

"You wouldn't know any of these people."

A LOVELY EVENING OF USELESS ERUDITION

My friend Tamara said her poems
didn't measure up, in the middling scheme, to
her sister's work as a scientist, which
stabs the feeling part of my brain
as one who reads & means nothing to the billions who don't,
but I spent the last night of the earth
in front of a cardboard fireplace
reading Walter Benjamin on Kafka which
led to Brecht which
led to a deeper look at the word 'parable' which
The Handbook of Literature linked
to didactic poetry, specifically not
Bryant's 'To A Waterfowl', which
I'd seen on my bookshelf earlier in the day, now
retrieved, though thinking not where the bird will land, but about
Angela's friend Dawn, who radiates beauty through kindness, but
doesn't read poetry, so
gave me the book, which
belonged to her grandparents, who
got it from, I can't say, but
the inscription in luxurious script reads:
Emma Bradford Stanton
  from Aunt Hattie
    Christmas, 1892

FALSE VACUUM

Her parents held 14 years

The US Army occupies 60 countries

Water prefers sea level

She had a few things to live for
each scar a story

Vitality runs fleet foot
  over the hill

Everyone at your local Book Shoppe
 is paying down a PhD

The Simpson's will rerun forever

Nothing a Fire Can't Fix

GUM CONTROL

A parking lot, across the street & down three blocks from the San Diego Convention Center, has been set aside for protesters of the Republican National Convention.

 Sounds so planned & canned—like ready to be filmed.

You can protest here in front of this brick wall, if the guys with rifles bother you, blindfolds will be provided & cigarettes compliments of Philip Morris.

Any last meal requests are at this time denied
due to funding cuts in the Head Start program.

All protesters will take buses to the parking lot, as not to stop traffic.

No flash photography.

Conspicuous port-a-potties will be provided.

No gum chewing.

Problems at past protests have stemmed from irresponsible gum owners.

This gum control will not be part of the GOP platform as Bazooka lobbyists donate too much money.

DISCOURAGEMENT

Try publishing a magazine every month for a year

Write a novel that few people want to read
Write six & your friends won't read them
              —Hey man, we've got our own problems

Put yourself out there like a Klown on public display

Drive 100 hundred miles to share your "poetry" with an audience of poets waiting their turn at the open mic

Time has a sneaky way, stumbling around like it's wasted

Stuff your size eleven feet in size seven shoes

Forage for approval

Dream about getting married or buying a home while living with a poet who thinks conventional wisdom is a conspiracy theory

Go without EVERYTHING

Fly under the poverty line like a missile under the radar
Time is desperate, lascivious, onerous

Starve inside the skin of a child with famine enforced by cheap labor

Sip coffee picked by bleeding fingers.   Vote.

Look in the mirror & deny the misanthropy etched in your pores
Name your blackheads after Greek myths

Eventually, one man will own the world

PORTENTS

Did you ever get the feeling you were riddled with cancer?
That every mole was a time bomb, waiting to go off?

That spider-bites were tumors aching to get out?

That your innards were like a garden hose kinked
or that perhaps the Marquis de Sade
was hiding up there disguised
as a rock-hard turd?

That your dendrites yellow as old newspaper crumbling
bequeath your memories to the wind?

Have you ever felt so flaky that you could feed your thoughts to goldfish?

That the twinge in your back signaled
the bones' ascendance, the skeleton's reich?

Death by six-hundred-million breaths

EASY TO UNDERSTAND

All the poet can do today is warn. Wilfred Owen.

We all know what's wrong
Wanda Coleman told us &
Jayne Cortez
Diane DiPrima knew
They told us
They told us in beautiful, clear language
Ferlinghetti & Ginsberg too
The poems were clear & easy to understand
Because we live in the world they describe
The poems were clear & easy to understand
Because they were our poems

They were our stories about our lives
They shouted in plain words
We said, Arrrrrr.
We said, Rrrrrrrrrr.

But we didn't know what to do

So we let the robber barons steal
We let the chasm that was the world grow

We let the controllers control
We let the liars lie &
The murderers keep on killing

Chomsky told us what to do, Joe Hill told him, Emma Goldman
told him & Tolstoy, Bakunin, Kropotkin & Thoreau told her

Get up—Get organized

TENDERNESS

Gilbert Sorrentino didn't like similes
(that wasn't a simile)
most seeming random

"The egg of tenderness will break in our hearts"

The Ming Vase of tenderness &
The favorite coffee mug of tenderness &
The first jalopy of tenderness &
The teenager's tender heart will break in our hearts too

The banana of tenderness will break
in three pieces
to share
with friends

The Neanderthal skull of tenderness will break
under the weight of our bloody cudgels

The long pushing out turd of tenderness will break inside the
rectum thus breaking our hearts & leaving us filled with melancholy

SPREADSHEETS

How many dishes washed?
How many single squares of toilet tissue used, folded, used, folded
How many trees?

How many linens in-n-out the wash & up on the line to dry?
How many million plastic microfibers lost at sea?

How much food shoveled in?
How much coffee?

498 elevator rides

$819.26 on gas is how far we got in two cars parked on the street

How many wine bottles recycled?
How many of whiskey & tequila?

44 of 51 Woody Allen films watched over a summer
2,582 books owned (owning me)
1018 hours worked

Our consumption of the earth taking the tigers with us & choking dolphins in the sea

Didn't use any condoms this year
Didn't cause any abortions[2]
Or set a balloon free

Bought two tires for the car
The blood of dinosaurs was our plan

Ne're a bullet fired, nor avalanche set in motion
Gave tears to a hurricane as the butterfly beat itself to death & fire moved the trees we breathe

---

[2] We had an abortion in 2001 when our fetus had congenital defects

Nothing a Fire Can't Fix

HUMANS USE TOOLS

An education professor
whose name I can't recall
advised me to remove the word

Hate

from my vocabulary in front of a class

And I realized how trivial my language

Hating traffic
Hating tax forms

So unmindful I was

But I hold this word in reserve
in my toolbox
against your apocalyptic values

hypocrisy
selfishness
greed
willful ignorance
short-sightedness

We are all looking for ways to put our genes forward,
so you use racism, sexism, homophobia, classism,
or carnivorous supremacy as a tool to limit competition

I've tried to banish this hateful crib sheet
on a rocket to deep space

As time passes & like Voyager 2 it leaves our solar system,
this passel of hates become harder to understand
harder to forgive

They are somewhat like the plastic Star Wars action figures
with which I battled the universe in 1977

put away
given away
thrown away
buried
decomposing
slowly
still recognizable
barely
somewhere
under the earth

POLAR EYES

When I think about Trump's image on your t-shirt cousin &
you flipping me the bird

I think of Trump the racist

of a refusal to rent a home to a black family
of a call to execute children falsely accused of rape
of calling Mexicans rapists & the racist wall

I think of the Southern Strategy, he inherited

His statement that there are good white supremacists
after one drove a car into a crowd

His followers flying the Confederate flag

Giving xenophobic Limbaugh a Medal of Freedom
like something straight outta Orwell

I think of Trump the misogynist

arguing that a husband can't rape his wife, using
fame to grab pussies & money to buy silence from prostitutes

I don't know if he fucked a kid on Epstein's island, but he wished
his friend the procurer well

I think of Trump the cheat

A man who cheats at golf, thinks nothing of cheating on wife after
wife after wife

The man who cheats at golf thinks nothing of cheating at elections,
accepting (never denouncing) help from Russians

I think of voter ID laws, gerrymandering, closed polling stations &

the sabotage of the mail

I think of Trump the "billionaire" jealous of trillionaires

Who only knows people as servants, pays his servants less per hour, & stiffs contractors

Who wants to end Social Security because it's communist

The man whose ideology is greed

allows corporations to dump waste in rivers, pushes coal to lower the quality of the air, for short-term profits

I think of Trump the liar

Who lied 20,000 times in three years, with his alternative facts & continuous attack on those who look closely

I think of fear-mongering hyperbole, mischaracterizations, half-truths, misdirections, white lies, dissembling, bald-face lies, & absurd conspiracy theories

I think of the people who will believe big lies

I think of Trump the dangerously petty egomaniac

Of the conflicts of interest
Of the tax returns

Ordering assassinations & trying to start a war with Iran
to move the news cycle off impeachment

I think of Trump the artless dodger

Who paid a doctor to get out of Vietnam
when 52,000 others died & killed
millions & lost their minds in the streets
when Reagan turned them out of hospitals

Nothing a Fire Can't Fix

When I think of the very stable genius who said,
"Man, Woman, Person, Camera, TV,"
I don't know what to think

I think of Trump the idiot

Who boasted of not reading books, who doesn't use email,
struggles with the teleprompter, & mispronounces "Yosemite"
because he doesn't care about a place we love

I think of the herd mentality
The hive mind
The cult

I think of the desperate maniac

sending Federal cops to create street theater
stoking dumb bikers & hate group militias to murder

I think of the failure who would have the White House boarded up
like the Taj Mahal

I think of his sham university & The New Jersey Generals

I think of the asshole who mocked a man's handicap

I think of the bully who uses name-calling because he has no policy

Let's think together about what it means to call a Senator
"Pocahontas"

Let's think about stolen land, poison, genocide, murder, & broken
treaties

I think of the admirer of dictators & autocrats
Who admitted he would refuse to accept the election results
& incited riot when it didn't go his way

I think of the incompetent fool who politicized health, stares at the sun, & denies science because it makes him look bad

"They say you can do too much testing?"

I think of the 200,000 dead
I think of their families

I think of Truman who said the buck stops here
I think of Trump who put the buck in his pocket

When I shared some of these things & you didn't think they were true, I thought it doesn't require much thinking, look them up

And when you said you don't see color,
       black & brown kids profiled by the cops
              should have the same option

I used to think people had one issue, like guns or abortion,
but the amount of ignorance that requires is astounding

Now I think anyone who stands for this is a racist who wants to put women back in their place & cares more about money than clean air & more about themselves than the least among us

THE EINSTEIN-BOHR DEBATE

The greatest argument of all time

Better than Wittgenstein v. Popper with the poker at Cambridge

Bertrand Russell smiles thinking of an old joke

The Thrilla in Manila

Mexico beats France in Pueblo

A sudden-death goal to the corner of the net
The sustained olé of 1.4 million synchronized hearts

Heisenberg & Bohr argued for uncertainty
Einstein & Shrödinger were determined

Einstein slams Bohr to the mat with a single photon; Bohr's down… up. He's up …oh… Bohr's got gravity… he drops gravity on Einstein

Still… our argument about buying a house eleven years back, as I lost mind & job, seems of more import—gravity multiplying as property values double

MORE SORRENTINOS

In the island of
　Your Heart,
Utterly banished I

On the patio of
　Your Heart,
a BBQ without coals

From the nest of
　Your Heart, pushed
I cannot fly

In the web of
　Your Heart, pinned
a spider's conscience sidles in for the kill

From the passenger seat of
　Your Heart, ejected
from a rollover crash

Nothing a Fire Can't Fix

BOREDOM

On the millionth death

Why are Americans such assholes, you ask?

When it's not about money, it's about boredom

They haven't found anything meaningful,
so they try to gap it with religion, with drugs

I can understand that, I ken pain
I've seen the movie that doesn't move…me

Some saved, by books, some done in

The bored are busy hating Jews or immigrants or transexuals
because it gives them something to do

Like congresspeople making laws

Like a child plucks a jointed segment of leg off an insect
I saw a bored kid whacking the heads off flowers with a stick

Once they get going that industrious efficiency that made their
bosses rich takes over

Conspiracies are a drug for people who think truth can be found
For those sad, unhappy people trying to ban books or abortions
for the men who start wars or cheat people out of a fair wage

You won't find meaning
because there isn't any

Meaning is in the things you make
with your hands, in the things you build
Meaning is in something you can hold up & say I did this

The bored confuse convenience with liberty
comfort with freedom
authoritarian with authoritative

They believe when they should test &
end making a Cause of privilege

Another stubborn old man chose to stop breathing

Nothing a Fire Can't Fix

MUD PIE & THE TITTY

A ten-year-old boy asks,
What happened to my youth?

FRUIT FLY

Fruit fly
thinks
it wants my wine

LONG DAY

Long lo-ooooo-nnn-g Da-yyy
Long lo-ooooo-nnn-g Da-yyy

Wa-aaaa-tch Tee Veeeeee
Wa-aaaa-tch Tee Veeeeee

Go-ooooo to sl-eeeeee-p

I HAVE UGLY GRAY DOG BALLS

I have ugly gray dog balls
I know this because
while stretching out before
taking a shower
I caught a glimpse of them
behind me in the mirror

Some of you feel catharsis as you read these lines, or if you're a guy you think

Do I have ugly gray dog balls?

If you're a gal you think

I'm blessed with this cheesy cellulite on my thighs, it's better than ugly gray dog balls

While contemplating this in the shower
I decide a little dry skin lotion will fix the sad sack right up
I massage it in, no lumps, & bend over for a look-see
Forget the ugly gray dog balls, I have a big red pimple on my ass

Again the possibility for catharsis,
the possibility to feel good about yourself
by watching others (me) suffer

Sto-o-o-o-p

I saw you thinking about checking your own arse in the mirror
It doesn't matter
if you're the hairy guy with two red pimples on your ass or the girl with cheesy cellulite thighs

It's okay

I am now your Klown

THE CURE

Angela felt a pinch of illness in her throat, so
I told her how this guy Steven at work said
to eat garlic, cutting it to awaken the anti-viral properties
which she did & after a second of burn on her tongue said,

At least I won't pass it on, since
no one will get close

BEACH TOWEL

A white beach towel, found
as pristine as the day you said we couldn't use it
set it in this drawer fifteen years back

BOOK FAIR

An old guy at the City College Book Fair
wearing a straw hat & Hawaiian shirt
asked the young woman at the AK Press booth
if she was a commie like "the other one" (PM Press)

We're not commies
We're anarchists

FREE THINKING

Georgie took Jami's book
She pulled for it back
I wrote his name on the board
                (Do I hate my job?)
He said,
                You can't teach anyway

There's so much chaos in my class

Free Speech & Seize the Day seem bad ideas

GRUMBLING

Angela has asked me again
not to walk around the house grumbling

        Shit & Fuck

She says my internal grief is contagious &
its expression blurting
brings her down

"Dump trucking"
                she calls it
dump
       dump
              FFFF

                Uhhhh

                KKKKKKKK

Nothing a Fire Can't Fix

NERVOUS BREAKDOWN

Today
I
lost
control
of
my
self
  crying later
when another adult approached me

The human concern dragged out tears, sobbing, my head lowered, eyes averted

I touched insanity

Know now what it means to plea that way

Part of me onlooking the action

                What is that guy doing?

Couldn't stop screaming
  Pushing the unwilling uncooperative
manifest of panic (a student)
to the door

A blackout
    to find the bad day 'come spectacle

Students want to know what's up?
Parents want to know what's up?
Teachers want to know what's up?
Principal wants to know what's up?

Self-sabotage, I thought, offering no reply

THE COSMOLOGICAL CONSTANT

I saw a lot of things today I would have liked to take pictures of,
she said

Did anyone else see them?

The (pink) elephant in the room
The cosmological constant
Einstein's "mistake"
an unrecognized truth
in a universe of dark matter
  war
  slavery
  pollution

The second sex
The invisible man
Pushing on our shoulders
Keeping us from implosion
Keeping an unrequited force from tearing us apart

KARMA

So this is what death looks like
Fog-smudged windshield
oncoming lights:

I'm on the mountainside coming down a divided silent road into
the lights at the point where the black ocean mouth bites the city:

Blood light ooze & smoke
shocklife feel the teeth shake
cold yellow blood cough
"The Hoax"

The road a rough black tongue to swim
throat swallow hope &
drown
sorrow in horizon
duodenum cloud bile &
slide to flatulent birth on distant shores
then drive

TIRED MIND

My brain feels limp
like an old penis with swollen balls

A sperm whale adrift,
loaded with ambergris

I can't remember books my journal says I read

I feel crushed by time
I blame work

I'm 40

Peter Boyle was 71

Reading the obituaries &
calculating the years
until I count the days

Thinking about Keats about Lautréamont…
      what they would have made

I remember the time I jabbed a steak knife into the meat of my
palm after burning the hand that held it on the toaster oven

NOW I AM THE CANCER

They are treating me like some obscure disease
cures have little effect on

The teachers', my colleagues', help
like chemotherapy

In the end, when I'm turning hard & black,
rotting within my skin
they will distance themselves
to protect their own bodies

I wish them well

QUITTING STUFF

I'm not saying quit smoking or quit coffee
or lay off that 750 ml bottle of Jim Beam,
but quit for a month

Show your addiction who's boss
  Then tell your boss you need a raise

Feminists aren't saying quit heterosexuality, but
like John Lennon said, "Sie liebt dich."

If you jerk to internet porn, try masturbating to lurid voter
pamphlets (politicians have been fucking you your entire life)

When Bush I announced the new world order, I was curious what
he was reading: Maimonides, Machiavelli, Ayn Rand, Leo Strauss

Fortunately, the dollar bill I was using as a bookmark caught my
eye —There, under the pyramid, the motto: "Novus Ordo
Seclorum" (New order for the ages)

I knew then what he'd been reading

Dick Cheney[y] has already explained the plan to trade liberty for
security to the reptile brain

When the Synapses started firing, the Amygdala grew nervous

   "¡Coup d'etat! ¡A revolution in the brain!"

"The Limbic System is holding us back!"

*Corpus Callosum pleads (like a sycophantic diplomat)
for rival hemispheres to join*

---

[y] Insert current political or religious leader

Nothing a Fire Can't Fix

> *"Medulla Oblongata marches from the south."*

The Occipital Lobe can see it all

> *¿What is Frontal Lobe planning to do without fear?*

Your hypothalamus convinces you of hunger,
but when was the last time you were really hungry?

FAST UNTIL YOU FAINT

Go on a hunger strike for an absurd cause
like the abolition of gravity
  or the end of global capitalism

> "I'm not eating another bite of ice cream
>   until you all give up your cars."

I conduct experiments on myself: Last month I ate:

Avocado, arugula, kale, & celery
Asparagus, broccoli, & lime
Spinach & chives, a gambit of peppers
Snap peas, wheat grass, & thyme
Nopalitos, tomatillos, kiwi, chard, & greens
Sprouts & basil, chard, chicory, oregano, olives, & peas
Parsley, scallions, cilantro, cabbage, peyote, endive, & beans
Honeydew, artichoke, cucumber, romaine…

Yes, my piss ran green

When was the last time you pissed outside, got your food 'round the back of the diner, slept in a cardboard box?

When was the last time you shit outside, used candles for light, huddled with your neighbors as earthquakes fell from the sky, searched the rubble for your son's arm so that you could bury him whole?

"Oh here it is…" looking like the last piece of KFC picked clean
by the dog… a splintered drumstick against an empty pot

CACEROLAZO-bang the bones of your dead son on a garbage can

Change friends like underwear (at least once a month)

If you don't like abortion, give condoms to high school girls
If you don't like sex… reread the line about lurid voter pamphlets

Go down on your knees often to meditate or copulate

Set up families in adjacent villages & hope the women don't
compare bambinos on market day

Plant a tree the day your daughter is born, threaten to chop it
down the day she loses her virginity, so there will be logs for the
fireplace when she wakes beside her lover

MY DAYDREAM

Begins at opposite ends of the couch
reading Whitman, aloud,
lines at random

I shall go forth   &   the drum strikes more convulsive

There's a secret word in Whitman, somewhere,
that will cause you to rise &
fall into me
with a kiss

COMMON SENSES

I can't figure out your watery love. Sex Pistols

The first time
I saw you
I understood
Stendhal
before Giotto's frescos
in the Basilica Santa Croce,
struck still
by the illuminated majesty of your face

An artist's trick
where the eyes look & the lips smile
only for me

Your time signature gripping cochlear hammers
to strike & strike my drums

A voice like the private concert
in Beethoven's skull
deaf & dumb
where syllables are notes
words, ideas
die, die, die
symphony

Every word like waking after my stop

Breathing you into my blood
fresh like iced blueberry on a main-vein to the brain
your skin, hair, & breath, your sweat

I know everything about you
like a dog that smells in stereo

A librarian in Alcatraz walking the tiers

Nothing a Fire Can't Fix

I looked for ways to touch you untouchable
like we were matter & anti-matter
in a large Hadron collider
loosing black holes upon the tiny universe
daring time to stop

like still images framed
by the window of a train

Inadvertent hip to hip
Reaching fingers met by a Trojan hand

Your imagination
Your favorite book
Your lips
Your hair
Your cotton
Your skin

Sebaceous

Always more

I want your wetnesses:

To lap at the aqueous pools where your eyes swim laps
to lick the plasma from your lips
Spit, snot, heme, & lymph
Nymph, I want the bile of your frustration
the Gastric acid of your rumbling tummy
the pus of every injury

Saliva divinorum

I'll make candles from your earwax &
watch over your rheum at night

Colostrum, holy city
where you breed, like Kali

like Nammu, the world's amniotic sea

Time can't trace me
It's all History (Ulrike spurned Goethe in 18-23)

It's not the 25 but the minutes
give me 15 & I'll put you in it

Practicare ante procreandi

Your magnetic field changed my course
as the center of your gravity called my name
off-balance, falling

My vomeronasal organ swells
as I bang on your doors & climb through your windows

Damn the eternal sunshine

I feel your temperature rising
a narwhal crashing through the ice

Beatrice
Selfish Jean

A few hours in Paradox
alone together

Rejoice—Ye who Enter

Nothing a Fire Can't Fix

THE HUMILIATION OF WORK

They asked me to sign this paper
giving the right to search me inside
their building & out

They want to search my car (~~i cross out that line~~)
thinking I want a job not to waive my civil rights

They want me to take a personality test,
though not sure why I need one
to file papers in alphabetical order

I must submit to a background check
fingerprints criminal credit history a drug test:

Have you used any drugs or alcohol in the last 30 days?
I drank 3 pints of Guinness at the bar each day for the last 30 days
What condition for was it prescribed?
                                                    The blues
Take off your clothes, underwear, socks, everything

The nurse knock-enters as I fumble with the strings of the hospital
pajamas, which always leave me feeling nakeder than naked
She escorts me down the hall…

Do not flush the toilet or the test is invalid

A guy with a broken arm shifts his gaze from my eyes to the plastic
cup to the floor, so he doesn't have to see my ass as I walk by

Have you got enough piss to make it past this line?

I must wait in the lobby for the boss to usher me through a cubicle
maze, I will not be able to find my way out of later

There are cameras everywhere

File cabinets full of debts, the names & addresses of debtors
I can't decide if a file gets lost behind the cabinet, whether the poor people will have to pay interest or if their debt will be forgiven

Individual Americans are like third-world countries

I find a ticket on my car in the parking garage, where I go to eat my lunch

Inside the complex, everyone has a cubicle but me

I file papers until my fingers bleed;
I file papers wiping the blood on a manila folder

A photocopied blood stain resembles Art—
I call this one "Pain, 105%"

My back hurts

I am too smart to be working here
my girlfriend says

I should be making more than 10 per hour

I try to use my mind for something besides daydreaming

I invent systems, use deductive reasoning to find the files with misspelled names

People who have held jobs longer than me think,

Get over it, you'll numb, callus, life is work–work is life

Nothing a Fire Can't Fix

GENERAL RELATIVITY

Allows for her to say something in one part of the universe &
for me to hear something completely different
in my own part of the universe

HEISENBERG'S UNCERTAINTY PRINCIPLE

You can never know
the velocity & position
of any electron.

Would my girlfriend have broke down
crying as her period attained requisite velocity,
if white wine had not been drunk & if
I hadn't been there to witness?

THE COUPLING CONSTANT

constantly coupling
inversely contortional
coupling constantly

MEDITATIONS

What an ignoramus is Death

Frank O'Hara killed by a dune buggy

lying in the sand &
with who?

   None of my business

To be hit by a dune buggy
like being caught dead in Utah

Traffic jams as drivers slow to gawk

Is this the spot?

The news isn't real
like viewing a body, still & hollow

How cool & clean & modern
How dark & serious & profound

WINE STAINS

Angela thinks I'm a wino
of some sort
pointing at the cabernet-colored
wine stain on my face

After scrubbing
it proves
a wound

which she, most likely, inflicted
in the night after that bottle,
so, she's right, again, it is

STRUMMER

*Every cheap hood strikes a bargain with the world, &
ends up making payments on a sofa or a girl...*

I bought a couch this week, the first piece of furniture that wasn't
handed down or found in an alley

I value truth, as I value soul in music

This is an elegy for a Man with Rotten Teeth
This is an elegy for The Only Band that Matters
This is an elegy for the man, the only band, the only father
we ever found

When an Iconoclast becomes an Icon, it's probably time to die

Oh… to die before we kill ourselves like Elvis
Oh… to die before we sell out
Oh… to die before we join the church
Oh… the rocknroll cliché

Strummer wrote a song about this, he wrote songs with words like
Sandinista & Sattamasagana

> *Death or Glory becomes just another story…*
> *[bom bom] Death or Glory becomes…*

The Hippies said,
    Never trust anyone over 30

The Punk Rockers said,
    Never trust a Hippie

When a punk rock friend of mine turned 40, she said,
    Never trust anyone under 30

Nothing a Fire Can't Fix

So far no one under 30 has said ANYTHING & we wonder if they ever will?

The Hippies' bellwethers lived fast & died younger

Jim, Janice, & Jimi forged The Curse of Turning 27

Before Kurt Kobain's death at 27, we debated whether he was a Hippie or a Punk Rocker:

> By the length of his hair, you'd have to call him a Hippie

> Yeah, but he got Pat Smear from The Germs in the band for punk rock street credibility

There's no compromise, just, a balance of extremes

My punk rock mentors lived fast, but failed to die young ——I lost a father & two far-out uncles this year

  Joey, Dee Dee, & now Joe Strummer forged

        The Curse of Turning 50

So like the Hippies I am now free to abandon my ideals for membership in the human race of patriotic consumption

Somebody sold a Clash song to a Jaguar commercial & another Clash song to a vodka commercial.

Did The Clash sell out?

The band that lifted me out of banality & catapulted me 25 years into the future & still going, still sounding fresh, still exhilarating when the needle hits the vinyl, cannot sell out. The man who sang, *I'm all Lost in the Supermarket* taught me that you are not your things & to bring my bullshit detector

I was orphaned when Strummer died at Xmas
  more like Nietzsche than Xist
  more like vitality than sickness

I'm talking about thinking & dancing

He named me & I took his name
  like it meant something
  like the name you get from the medicine man

    Police walked in for Jimmy Jazz...

The Hippies lost faith & bought Mercedes

Strummer sang: *He who fucks nuns will later join the church...*

I do not believe in heroes or mourning or death
  only in wakes & potlatches & ascetic austerity

I believe in Monk-like retreats & that different rules apply on tour

And I, like Joey & Dee Dee, & Joe, am on tour 365 days a year

I didn't cry when Joe died

I played The Ramones 24 hours when Joey died
I played The Clash 48 hours when Joe died

I got drunk but I didn't cry

    From every dingy basement on every dingy
    street, I hear every dragging handclap over
    every dragging beat...

If it's a contradiction to water your mentors while stating resolutely that you don't need heroes, so be it

I also contain multitudes

Nothing a Fire Can't Fix

MY UNCLE, MY MOTHER'S BROTHER

The hippie with long red hair in a fading photograph named
his dog after Jethro Tull

My uncle, the practical joker, balanced
bowling balls on the door to drop on his brothers

My uncle taught me to throw a spiral forward pass stretching
my short fingers across the laces

My uncle took me to Knott's Berry Farm offering
a hit of marijuana before the roller coaster

Didn't push when I said, No thanks

My uncle hitting home runs at the family picnic,
Fourth of July

My uncle, the father of cousins I rarely see;
youngest brother to my mother

My uncle, the user
got his jaw broke burning
the angels on a speed deal

My uncle, the Cat Burglar of Ocean Beach took
my ten-year-old cousin to rob a trailer counseling
You can take just one thing

My uncle, in jail

My uncle, the rumor

My uncle, who after a massive heart attack,
climbed the highest rock on the mountain

My uncle, whose unexpected presence at Xmas, sent

auntie into convulsive tears of joy

My uncle, the dumpster diver
found a gold necklace for his girl &
got himself a 3-piece suit at the thrift store
(vest too small, pants for high water)

My uncle, who believed in angels
had his ashes dumped in the sea

A SKIRMISH

The Skilled Nursing Facility ("Sniff")
wasn't designed to accommodate visitors

the two tiny beds
share one TV

ABC, NBC, ABC, NBC
OFF, ON, OFF, ON
Louder Mute Louder Mute

Patients trade potshots across the curtain
pulled when the Certified Nursing Assistant comes
to change the diaper

GILA BEND

The desert is full of stories

Mary's dad told me about the bunkhouse, accessible by horseback,
he & his buddies constructed of cast-off junk on the dry wash

Baling cotton at the truck stop, a buck a bale
or a buck a day, I forget

Getting drunk with the boys, age 12

There was one guy outside Gila Bend on a farm
musta had a thousand snakes in a pit
30 feet deep with chicken wire over the top

He milked 'em, sold venom to the government

> Did I show you
> my draft card?

Blew a thousand bucks in Reno...

Sitting in his beat armchair, green, with worn-through armrests, TV
on, Mr. Coffee brewing in a pot, he could tell this story about
growing up, boundlessly, because he lived there more than here

STRING THEORY

Asserts that
    reality
is
music
played on
    fundamental
strings
whose
vibrations
determine
    the shape of
things

vibrations
    resonate
like Parker's
alto
  changes
 mood

A POEM FOR JANICE JORDAN

Begin with a political platform embedded under the skin in ink

I never got a tattoo because I never believed in anything,
but she is practically sleeved with belief

Gonna talk about race & sex & class when the economy is stuck on
prosperity, since the majority is still a minority when it comes to
getting paid

How many meetings can a single mother attend?

Free Mumia at 6
Police sensitivity training at 5
Stop the war at 4
Ban the bomb at 3
Stop the presses at 2
Fund the Zapatistas at 1
Unless house the homeless on Thursday &
attend a gay marriage every Sunday

Save Peltier & Big Mountain & the whales by putting a cap on
CEO's profits. Tax the fuck out of our sins.

"And just because we legalize hemp, doesn't mean we have to
smoke it."

Ban the bomb // ban the ban // ban the banners of books // wave
the banner of peace & freedom // like kids at a rock show // with
clenched fists in the air keeping time to the music // shouting
Power to the people! Power to the people!

What are you running for? // What are you running for?

We like your energy but have to vote for the same lethargy
if we vote 'cause you ain't viable without deep pockets

Nothing a Fire Can't Fix

Listen buster, if she had a hundred million dollars, she wouldn't waste it on TV commercials

Can't explain why the border should be torn down & feminism could mean women asserting themselves like women in a sound bite anyway

CA Propositions 187 & 209 are examples of institutionalized greed

The difference between Democrat & Republican
like the difference between two right hands confirming a dirty deal

The war chest is empty
but resounds as you beat on it like Tarzan

The guerrilla fighter // the rocknroller // the bread bringer // the woman who takes men to the mat & pins them by their ears with rivets of common sense // the student of Emma Goldman // has got your back in every crisis // the leader who follows // the truth like one of the converted // the speaker who listens // the faithful atheist // who communes with the Aztecs on the solstice

Imagine a city where the only rule is respect & vote

DRAGGING MY ASS THROUGH THE DAY

I saw the best minds of my generation destroyed by work, overfed, somber, dressed to the nines...

Dragged through the jungle by my balls, graduated the University of Middle Passage (UMP) put my own soul on the block, sold myself down river to work, I have no overseer to blame but desire

Looked emancipation in the face 'til the whipcrack of the clock pulled me back to work chewing the stale dream of Roosevelt's reparations

Social Security...has run out... 65 , 67 , 72 , 80? Little old ladies at the welfare office'll be calling me "Silver Fox" when I'm 80

Boss rewards my good work by letting me come in on Saturday (overtime under the thumb of time)

So now I'm Dragging My Ass Through the Day, 'cause I refuse to be <u>just</u> a slave, stayed up late looking for every minute I lost

Got books to read, damnit I feed on books & I'm starving in a land of famine

Dragging My Ass Through the Day
Didn't somebody fight a war that freed the slaves?
Better read the fine print on the 13th amendment

Slave to rent, slave to stomach, destroyed my health looking for health care, everywhere slaves to fashion, slaves to distraction, I'm a slave to "meaningful" things like sending my kid to college

At the mercy of my energy, working to buy the drugs I use to get through working

Una siesta would be simpatico

Nothing a Fire Can't Fix

What happened to the promise of technology?

A sleepworker stumbling in somnambulance, a deadman—mortgaged my soul for a coffin

How many hours did you spend working?
How many hours did you spend fucking?

Instead of Fuck You, I'm gonna say, You Work
Instead of Mother Fucker, I'm gonna say, Your Mother Works

Dragging my Ass Through the Day, wrote this poem on my 15-minute break

Do you know how many lunch hours it takes to read In Remembrance of Things Past? ALL OF THEM

Got mental emphysema from my cubicle coal mine

I got games to play // things to say // wars to stop // socks to hop // roads to trip // pirate ships (arrggg)

On Sunday, I pull up a bottle of wine pull the shades & pretend I'm in an opium den flophouse with my lover

Don't apologize for calling at midnight
Don't apologize for dancing in the street with piñatas
Don't apologize for humping & screaming while you hump, upstairs neighbor girl, you rocked my ceiling like a wet dream

Talk to the movie screen, shout dreams, bathe in streams

Let the babies cry in the theater // Let the children play in the street // Tell those goddam teenagers back in the garage to turn the amplifier up to eleven

I will never let living be an excuse, I refuse slavery & drag my ass through the day

ANXIOUS BEATS

I peer into the toilet
with fear & some anxiety
at the bloody aura oozing from the matter

—Am I dying?

With relief & some delight,
I recall the meal shared:

Baked tofu marinated with ginger & orange, kale, & roasted beets

A candle between us
forks clanking plates to keep time

These lines help me
remember the flavors &
your lingering fart in bed

The accretion of joy
after so many meals shared
adding by 1s by 3s by 30s
these 30 years

Nothing a Fire Can't Fix

THE CUBE

I sit & stare
& sit & stare
& stare & sit
& type & sit & stare
& mouse & sit &
sit & stare & scrutinize
the numbers & sit & stare
& listen to Abbey Hoffman
on headphones, thinking
if he saw me sitting here
he'd say
        Asshole
& I sit & stare &
type & mouse & sit &
on my 15-minute break
I walk the yard & sit & stare

THE TYRANNY OF PANTS

When I step into my apartment
after a long day in THE CUBE
I strip off my pants

As if boxer shorts equaled freedom

As if in throwing off your pants,
you could throw off the humiliation of work

Since my car got stolen, I ride my bike downtown to THE BUS

When I mention the hope never again to own a car, my dad says
I'm acting like a Martyr

I prefer Commutyr

The people of THE BUS seem more tired, more beat, more sullen
Most people in THE CUBE do not ride the bus

People step onto THE BUS at dawn with sleep-crusted eyes
People roll into THE CUBE around nine pre-loaded on Starbucks &
propped up on cigarettes

BUS & CUBE people alike feed on shitty, albeit fast, food
(on the bus & in the cube) not spilling enough on shirt fronts
to keep from growing slowly fat

The system's rent, its credit (its interest) its bills
hang on us like a dress on a drowning girl

I want to quit my job
like I quit my pants

I want to feel like I feel after three highballs of scotch
without drinking three highballs of scotch

Nothing a Fire Can't Fix

A sage once said, "Work is stupid, it makes you tired."

Mario, a coworker, gets up at 3:30 to cross the border
EVERY DAY

This 83-year-old black woman on THE BUS worked 28 years as a maid at the Hotel San Diego until it was razed for condos

"28 years of mopping & smiling," she says.

The Mexican dude on the next seat says, "I have five childrens."

"You Mexicans are smart people," she says. "You work hard."

His lower back demures

On my iPod,
Joseph Campbell said, "Follow your bliss"

Bill Moyers said something like, "A hero should sacrifice bliss for family."

I go to work; I decay
getting stupider by the minute
as brain cells saturated with account numbers
slough off to nothing

like the tyranny of pants

SCHADENFREUDE

Coming to the office, a red ambulance

Holding the door for the paramedics,
I saw my boss wheeled out on a gurney

Upstairs my coworkers catch me fighting a smile

"It was her gall bladder," one says. "She'll be okay."

I let the smile free

To do as it wanted,
needed

Nothing a Fire Can't Fix

GRAVEYARD SHIFT

> *Anyone showing insufficient grief could be accused of killing the man through witchcraft. Pagan Kennedy*

Late-night worker at a "prayer station"
on Ground Zero reports that God is sad

Even as a non-believer, this idea rubs wrong

It's hard to believe a god would care
though if it did, you could imagine the morass
of having to be sad all the time

The billions of tiny losses every day

More likely your god is too busy to be sad,
which is why no one has seen him for two thousand years
Laughing at the joke set in motion
by a game of Risk™ with Zeus, Kali, & Thor

3,000 of my fellow citizens are dead & that I don't care enough disturbs me

I know I'm supposed to, but I don't, feel enough

I don't have sadness to lay a blanket
against the cold injustice of the world

I think of people in Palestine, Afghanistan, Iraq
        Post-colonial chaos in The Philippines
                State-sponsored terror in Indonesia

So maybe I'm overwhelmed by sadness

I see the comfort that janitors & millionaires think they've earned & with that… the risk

Cecil says "indifference is a bad position to hold"
as if it was an intellectual choice

He thinks I live in a mental ghetto
where the books I read tell me how to feel

    I feel like Camus' Stranger

He asks what makes me sad
Trained by movies—manipulated by music & juxtaposition

    I feel like K in the shadow of the castle

The coming war fills me with rage because I can't stop it
Sadness feels like a reason not to do anything

SINGULARITY

Americans compete toward infinitesimaltude

Zeno's infinity between every point broken by fundamental strings

The infinite universe measured at 13.7 billion years

No original thought since Einstein, my high school teacher said
Poets dream infinity / Scientists of symmetry

Einstein said, "Pure mathematics is, in its own way, the poetry of logical ideas."

Artaud said logical ideas were absurd (Poetry, he called pigshit)

Marx attacked Proudhon & Fourier
Don't jail the Anarchists until the Fascists are beaten

You are a particle & a wave

Ptolemy, Hobbes, & Kant helped build the church of monotheist robber barons.   Gödel was incomplete.

I don't believe in heroes, rather honor research assistants & backing bands.

Where would Billie be without Lester or Ché without Fidel?

The NY Yankees, The NY Dolls
The Harlem Renaissance, The Harlem Globetrotters

The founding fathers created checks & balances
to prevent the executive from becoming a monarch

Hawking said a spinning black hole doesn't collapse to a singularity

Bukowski said, "Don't try."

DEATH'S COUSIN

Am I the same person inside that boy
standing on 2nd watching the kickball game unfold?

I remember being inside that boy like a man in a bear suit
looking out

Am I the same consciousness?

The cells from those days have died
Have been replaced

My old leather belt lets
my pantaloons slip off my hips
I don't recognize the black hairs on my forearm
Or this constellation of melanin
Nor these withered skeleton hands

The pain, though, in my back is an old friend &
in the morning I recognize my cock
like a slobbering dog turning circles to greet me at the door

Will I disappear?

Shrinking as I am
become so small as to be
unrecognizable

I remember this brain, some of these thoughts,
unfortunately, are not a total stranger's

Decay is the enemy of humankind

¡VOILA!

And now it's raining on a genus of trees belonging to the family
Simaroubaceae & now it's snowing
A wind over here
There a moment of calm
The sun is out
Now rain, again
Over here
And there is a Picasso
A real one
  Cost 60 million
Here's a cool mill in my pocket
There Brussels sprouts
which I like
basted with olive oil, roasted

Is poetry
prestidigitation?

The sum & go
of time & line

Here is a blue whale
  its majesty
beached on the shore-less shore

FOIA REQUEST

Paul Blackburn lamented in 1954 that the world was losing its individuals to the machine.

A Google search will not prove you an individual.

You are like the FBI agent who watched John Lennon, watching your tv.

You are like the FBI agent who watched Dr. King, watching the protestors out in the street.

You are like the FBI agent who watched Albert Einstein, tool of a system that can't abide change.

You are the FBI agent who infiltrated the Quaker meetinghouse to monitor conscientious objection.

Judge a person's character by the content of her FBI file.

Abbie Hoffman, full of Haight. Sami Al-Arian, a patriot. Eldridge Cleaver, like a shotgun cradled in the crook of a strong arm. Assata Shakur…[knowing grin] Julia Butterfly Hill, like a redwood. Judi Bari, the bomb.

Ward Churchill said, "Put yourself in close proximity to men who face death."

We value guilt-by-association the way they value greed.
We value weird thinking & audacity of the deed.

A chattel slave has the right to slit his master's throat. Humans of the twenty-second century will wonder why we didn't kill our bosses & landlords more often.

We laugh when the cabal is jailed by laws they felt above; we scratch our heads when the next cabal pardons their excess.

Nothing a Fire Can't Fix

The difference between Democrat & Republican like the difference
between two right hands confirming a dirty deal.

I do not mean to bring violence to bear against men
(the corporate state has a monopoly on murder.)

I mean to destroy the institutions that breed exploitation
by any means necessary…

Wage slavery   Representative democracy

Screw the porntopia of the patriarchs:
Xtianity & Hollywood

Paul Blackburn called for a song from the gut that would help a
man stand a better chance of standing when it was necessary to
take a stand.

I'm asking you to sing like Martin Luther King
& dance like Weird Al Einstein.

THE SILENCE

There's a jet coming in &
the ringing in my ears

damage done

This silence isn't the absence of sound

An empty space
in head

in gut

a lack
a nil

Another jet
A car driving by outside
My upstairs neighbor's stupid voice, "Oh cool."

With the right pickup & amplifier,
thoughts make sounds

a cry coming to be
a gasp fading away

SMALL TALK

*I spent a day among normal folks recently &
realized that I no longer speak their language*

A couplet of free verse I wrote 15 years ago still terrifies me

Walking to the corner store, I wondered what it would be like
to walk past the library, watch football on a Sunday afternoon,
drink Budweiser, play poker with the guys, go fishing, talk about
boobs

(Don't get me wrong, I admire boobs, silently)

Maybe I could own a car, shop for new clothes, wear a watch,
listen to the radio, own a house, & worry about money

But would I have to hate books, vegetables… thinking?

Would I have to get pissed about traffic, fear thy neighbor, & drink
bad coffee because it's convenient?

Convenience would become one of my values
along with banality & even just plain dumb
feels easy trying it on like shoes at the mall

The guy picking through the garbage
for aluminum cans
is wearing the local team's colors
knows the quarterback, knows the score
of yesterday's game

He laughs, discovering some significant object

Extending a dirty hand
to a partner I hadn't seen
to help him from the dumpster

THE KISS

> *now we have only kisses,*
> *like little furry bees. Osip Mandelstam*

The initial breath of our first kiss
will hold the length of a feature film
with all its rising action, climax & denouement
our teeth like extras aching for screen time
our tongues stunt-doubles on a coffee break
ahead of the big scene where they'll ride motorcycles
down the esophagus into the stomach

The flickering light from our first kiss
will send the baby roaches scurrying to crevices
behind the baseboard

The static surge from our first kiss
will short the power grid causing a statewide rolling blackout

And chain-reaction of discreet kissing

which will engulf distraction, cease commerce, & grind to halt the machine freeing people from the prison of their lives—out of the dark onto the street—neighbors will speak for the first time, about…

Our first kiss, my lips on yours
sharing a secret in the playtime tent of your hair

Our first kiss, an invitation for fingertips to graze skin like
pillowy sheep denuding a hillside

Our first kiss by the factory wall

Projecting winter-ocean-panorama
vistas of bliss
blinding, thought-stealing

Nothing a Fire Can't Fix

pain-vanquishing bliss

Our first kiss
will make us whole like
vampires supped on blood

Our first kiss will race the blood over the Black Hills through the Shenandoah across the Great Plains of our bodies to the cities of our minds

Our first kiss in the Empire State Building
grasping the secret dirigible port in the steeple like
Kong beating the drum of his breastplate

Kiss me in the Okefenokee
 on a snowy slope at 3.2%
 on a grassy knoll
Kiss me in a St. Louis project
 or The Beverly Hilton

The cryogenic chamber of our first kiss
with ages falling around us
a space without time
—the 20s roar
—the Depression lifts
—Wars are fought but for what?
—Skirts rise like housing prices, before they fall
—the moon gets walked on

Your kiss like the captain of a press gang
a leather sap behind the ear
shanghai i into service

Your kiss is Washington's cherry tree
(in full blossom)

Your kiss is Paul Bunyan's ax &
John Henry's hammer

Your kiss caused so many things to get lost in the cushions of the couch—an earring, a button, one sock

Our kiss
fits right in
between two volumes of poetry in a lonely library stack &
re-writes the sonnets with your name

It's easier to mediate
on kisses than levitate
looking down on the geometry
of human discourse
cut by roads dizzies
the green squares
triangles
rectangles
circles
rows
rivers like blue snakes
lakes in tear shapes
up here you realize that fog is nothing but clouds on the ground
floating around
inhaling your exhale

When your lips pull back—
I hope but briefly—
to draw oxygen instead of CO_2
I think of the hours spent like Scott Fitzgerald waiting for a note
looking vainly to the universe for a sign
counting maddening coincidences as they mount
I lean forward almost falling
as you feint toward then pull back

A cod with the hook set, my heart thrashes on the deck of your trawler

Come visit me in banishment
in my corn field

Nothing a Fire Can't Fix

at Manzanar
in Leavenworth
on Alcatraz

Follow the buffalo road to the salt lick

Kiss me on the subway
on the L or the BART

By chance in an elevator

```
                Atop
      world       the
       the       Ferris
       atop     Wheel
            stopped
```

On a divan, nervously
where elbows click like billiards

With breath like raspberries
 or garlic
 or tobacco
 or rye

Pressed against the jukebox
Rolling from a bonfire in the sand

Our teeth clash like north & south
Our first kiss manumits
the slave of my desire
freeing me to be less stupid & awkward

On the bus
On a bridge

In a shabby stairwell
peeled paint become redwood bark
 the unchallenged stillness of an ancient grove at Sequoia

—the tension—frightening footfalls echo from a floor above like
brown bears coming to steal our picnic

Your nails carving a better Rushmore into my back
with Thoreau, Goldman, Tubman, & Twain
in place of the slaveholders, reluctant emancipator, & would-be
imperialist

Clinging like teenagers melting on a beach like
some old white dude in a red Maserati clutching his last blue pill

The oblivion of our kisses
caused us to miss
—Columbus's intentions
—Jackson's smallpox interventions
—Oppenheimer's homicidal invention

There's a genocide hidden in our kiss

where entire peoples are displaced
red-skinned bodies stacked in bones
around the feet, ankles, knees & rising
past the shapely buttocks
your hips my back our ribs
your breast my chest
shoulder deep in gore but oblivious in our kiss

Sending hands by rail
over the corpses of uncounted Chinese
to remote regions of your body
dynamiting mountains of resistance
crossing rivers of guilt like
Clark & Lewis in their stupid canoe
manifest destiny
dragging my hands like
a piano in a covered wagon
trying the Oregon trail of your legs
to meet your ugly feet
which I will bathe in the cold Pacific—

Nothing a Fire Can't Fix

beautiful ugly weary feet that walked halfway round the world

I'd become a politician to kiss you as a baby

Our kiss like crazy brothers taking flight in an insane idea

the dynamo of industry
feeding the fires of commerce
the flesh & blood of the land
turning dirt into money & smoke
choking the air
leaving the waters undrinkable
the acidified rain
erodes the strip-mined mountaintops
surrounding Stumptown

Our kiss invented the internet
transplanted a heart

Our kiss melts polar ice &
makes the plastic oceans rise

Our kiss vanishes islands

Our kiss come down to Georgia like a devil to train a death squad

Our kiss employs the spies
of our ears & eyes & readies our hearts & hands to kill
anyone coming between our lips

Stock traders speculate
Barnum hawks tickets &
billionaire hedge fund managers bet we will break

Our kiss plays blues licks & jazz riffs
in a cool quartet with our heart on drums

rocknroll, disco, punk, pop, & hip hop ebb & flow like the tides on
Lake Michigan by the moon's pull, snapping fingers & singing:

shoop shoop shoop shoop
shoop shoop shoop shoop

The roof of your mouth is the shelter my tongue needs
Your tongue in my cheek like an inside joke

peck smack smooch

Blame the French when it gets dirty
Napoleon, you mad fool selling New Orleans

Jambalaya & a crawfish pie & fillet gumbo

un bisou
un beso
um beijo

kisu   kiss you

Our first kiss sews a green garden with strawberry seeds

Mouth-to-mouth resuscitation after a summer swim too far

In the hayrick by lightning flash, I glimpse your face
standing like an oak tree with mistletoe in your hair

In the back seat of a car, Kenickie knew more about kissing than Klimt

Gojira, Rodin, Brancusi

Making out, necking, locking lips, & swapping spit

Mamo signed her name with kisses that smelled of lavender
xo xo xxx

A REEF

coffee
cognac

odor of old bread toasting

tiny bits of matter riding currents of air
fall to dust

What life lives on you
swims in sick room sweat
held close to skin
accreting layer by layer
like coral

WHEN PHYSICISTS TALK ABOUT GOD

Karl Marx said materialism leads to deism,
an atheism for slack-jawed yokels

Like a poet groping for a word: "World"   "Universe"
                           "Reality"   "Existence"

Nothing seems adequate

When physicists talk about god, they mean nature or what they
don't yet understand
	Namedropping Jehova more than ministers

The atheist physicist doesn't believe in what she doesn't
understand

God plays dice with electrons on a quantum craps table
Probability is everywhere

Theoretical physicists are looking for a theory
"about an inch long" to "read the mind of god"

LISA will take a picture of HIS filthy nails
in the million trillion billionths of a second after the big bang,
proving existence snapped into being

What if god paints her fingernails pink?

A meeting of the branes————An umbilical cord

A genesis————apocalypse
         tug-o-war
Matter moving forward in time
              resembles anti-matter moving backward
         The collision is energy

Entropy takes care of itself

TRAIN WHISTLES

My grandma said that train whistles remind her about her Papa who, when he got fed up with his girls (a wife & 3 daughters), would

> "Grab a handful of boxcar."

He'd been a fireman on the trains, stoking coal for the steam engine. He struck oil at Signal Hill, where he found these candlesticks left by some pioneers, but his partner ran off with the money. His partner left him flat.

OBLIGATIONS

I was bothered this morning & last night by my family obligations. I didn't want to rub Angela's feet. I was washing the dishes & almost lost it as she gave directions to clean this & don't get water on the floor & close that box... then (angelically), "You can go to the bar tonight."

DOING JUST ONE THING

I've always had trouble
doing just one thing

Just now, for example

As I was folding the laundry
I cracked a beer

A few towels in
I wrote this in my head

>   Washcloth, washcloth
>   Dishtowel
>   Bath towel

Nothing a Fire Can't Fix

HELPER

A man in a wheelchair
haled one of my students

Can you hold this cup for me son?

It was a waxy paper cup from 7/11

He did

My student felt the warmth
looking at it, curiously, not knowing the word 'urine,' thinking in
images, groping for language

the amygdala switches the senses on

Suddenly, you see a bottle at the curb, you notice the trash strewn
all around, spilled food, flies, soiled rags

A siren, ambulance, echoes down the block

The acrid smell comes on like two shots of tequila,
the dry wet smell pushes into his nose
as it crawls up into his mind

Mudbricks itself in like

your first kiss
your first corpse
your first failure

He saw the man's feet swollen, a chiaroscuro of scabbed & open
sores

He saw then the man's pants gathered low on the sidewalk
He saw the black hairs, the ugly dick
the dribbled wet spot

Can you help me pull up my pants?

He did

My student pulled this man's pants up around his hips

That was very kind of you, I said. You should always help if you can, but next time, be more careful. He could've had a needle in his pocket. You could have gotten poked

I saw in his face that there wouldn't be a next a time
that even the most charitable among us have limits

I saw a naïveté dissolve
          a butterfly snatched by a mockingbird mid-flight

This wouldn't happen in my country, he said
We take care of people, we have hospitals

Most people here, I said, say people should take of care of themselves

Nothing a Fire Can't Fix

SLUMMING FOR KIDNEYS

My bones are plastic
My teeth are gold

Your body wears out when you get old

I'm looking for a man who will sell me his eyes &
a dick transplant to improve my size

Slumming for kidneys
Whatcha gonna do?
Mine are shot &
You got two

I smoked my lungs & I drank my liver, but
my money found a willing giver

In the poorest province, I got a new start
Spoke with a mother at "Extra Kid Mart"
The youngest was really smart
The middle child a genius of art
I bought the one with the generous heart

FALLING ASLEEP IN FRONT OF THE TV

You didn't hear the wind howling
through the streets & rattling the doors
because you don't hear that good &
the TV was on, loud
because you don't hear that good,
nor did you hear the rain
on the roof all night
because the TV was on, loud, &
I wonder if you used it
all these years living alone
to protect yourself from silence,
from guilt, from regret
As long as the TV is on, this loud,
you won't miss the thoughts that never formed

GO SLEEP OFF THE BOOZE NIGHT

Let the sun step over your road-killed carcass

Time will push the jangle bang bone cart of your body through the years

Gonna let Art play you like a leap frog?

Riddup

Go sleep off the booze night

Your sleep? Waking flip-flop. Your dreams? The up-close pillowcase smell of bar-smoke dreams spilled out of nostrils & mouth holes in moments of sad laughter

Go sleep off the booze night

RACE BASED ADMISSIONS

The supreme court split 5-4 today on whether prisons should use race as a criterion for admission.

The executive branch came out against the policy adding that they would not support legacy admissions either. Just because your father got in a good prison doesn't mean you should.

A warden in Massachusetts, asked why there aren't more women in prison, suggested the phenomena had something to do with brain physiology.

A spokesmodel for the Texas state prison system argued that their Affirmative Action program had been a striking success.

> "Our minority outreach has proven successful. While only 4 of 10 Texas citizens are minorities, in the prison system we have achieved a remarkable 7 of 10 rate for blacks & latinos."

Recruiters around the country have already been delivering the Taser Achievement Test to boys as young as six & girls in handcuffs.

The Texas prison spokesmodel added that they would like to expand the Phi Beta Capital Punishment program to reach more retarded & impoverished citizens in the years to come.

Nothing a Fire Can't Fix

DECOHERENCE

Our wave functions entangle
Flop-housing in the Opium Den
Shades pulled low like sleepy eyelids shutting
Case of shiraz & a corkscrew
Vibrating in unison
Mail carrier pushes a pile of junk mail through the slot
Landlord leaves three notes—yellow, blue, then pink
We hide under dark covers
TV broke // no radio // phone disconnected
Loteria candle burnt to the nub

Walden Pond
Kaczynski's shack
A crippled hermit's cave

Our cat eats the roaches that slip under the door

The worn grooves of my desert island disks crackle—
Hank Williams, Billie Holiday, Joy Division, & The Germs

The slightest interaction with the outside world will separate us
You're thinking about going back to work
We fall out of synchronization

Like a man jumped from an 8-story window

Lost to each other

We decohere

THE REALITY

End with couch sitting
Klown suit, boxed
Banana peels compost in a steaming heap
Not caring about getting a blow job these days, much
The caress of a healing hand, needed
Time is running for its life
The surveillance camera in the back pocket of my jeans follows me, everywhere
The dossiers have been compiled, clicks without meaning
The surgeon is a robot, like the car, like everything
You are alone
With wooden shoes out of fashion
There's still nothing to spend your money on

Nothing a Fire Can't Fix

HUMMING

Angela getting ready to go
packing a lunch
humming, as she does, like the strum
of a tuned guitar

Melodious

She says unconscious
her humming,
pointedly, not quite song

I shouldn't mistake it for happiness, she adds
though it makes me

Our nephew who she cares for
days while his parents work
joins in

Hm hm hm hm Hmmmm

THE APRÈS GARDE

Lallygagging onto the scene
broom & mop
moping—heads hung—they aren't even the lost generation

All the good ideas stomped like carnival detritus
rats dazzled by bits of string
thread the nest with sinews of flesh
a log cabin of severed left arms
Dalí's skull with a mustache painted by Duchamp
Lorca's heart fossilized in Franco's stomach

Perhaps it's better to starve

Would you rather be poignant enough to kill or
be made vapid by fame?

Voluntary poverty being a myth, rather than a legend

What would Art mean without Capitalism
to buy her drinks & tell her she's pretty?

You could use the scabs on Johnny Thunders' arms as a bomb
shelter, but he couldn't

You could use Dee Dee Ramone's busted synapses as snitches in
the police state of your mind

You could leap from a window like

Chet Baker
               (unless he was pushed)

Like Unica Zurn
               (in self-defenstration)

Nothing a Fire Can't Fix

Like Jeanne Hébuterne
 Bacon, Casagli
Francesca Woodman
   Lembit Oll, Allyn King
   Capucine
 Christy, Gildo
 Deleuze, Hirsch
Kocsis
    Gale

Like Bohumil
    Hrabal
Arihiro Hase
   Donny Hathaway
      Pascal
         Hartman

Testing the tensile strength of a man

   Nedbal's fall from the opera house
Herko's grand jeté
   Edward Armstrong waving from the 13th floor

Townes Van Zandt wondered what it would be like to fall... he said

Hudsucker & Lisbon fell down frames of celluloid
so Alice down the rabbit hole

John Waters made a film about Diane Linkletter
Frida Kahlo painted Dorothy Hale

the final resting pose

The act of thinking about suicide might help you span a terrible night, Nietzsche claimed... Bukowski wrote *Poems Written Before Jumping Out of an 8-Story Window* but never did

RUSHMORE

ronald reagan ronald reagan
on rushmore on rushmore
ronald fucking reagan
ronald fucking reagan
on rushmore

CERTAINTY

Every church began as a gang
Every universe with a silent bang
Every swan is not white
Every day has followed every night… so far
Every life ends in dirt
Every joy turns to hurt

TWAT

It is the war that never ends
It goes on & on my friends
Some people started bombing them
knowing what it was &
they'll keep on bombing them forever
just because…

Nothing a Fire Can't Fix

THE LAST PIECE OF SHIT

Toilet seat warms to body temp
The last piece of shit refuses to discharge
like that constipated bullet in the suicide gun

Acknowledgments

Drunk Blues in Revival: spoken word from Lollapalooza 1995

Drunk Blues on the Incommunicado CD Exploded Views 1995

Is 74 Old Enough? appeared on Instagon http://sandpiper.ccc.ccd.edu/instagon 1996

Inside-out Love Story in Cupid 1997

Ugly Gray Dog Balls in City Works 1997

Angela in Damaged Goods 1997

Chiapas 45 in Will Work for Peace 1999

Espresso ex Machina in Map of Austin Poetry 1999

The Pig Ritual, Is 74 Old Enough, & Gum Control in Map of Austin Poetry 2000

A Poem for Janice Jordan in Map of Austin Poetry 2001

The Free Way & Denial in Get Rich Slow Scheme 2002

Tell the Revolutionary Court, Strummer, Small Pox & Dragging My Ass Through the Day in City Works 2003

Anarchist Think Tank in Boom v.1 2004

Stuckism in the San Diego Poetry Annual 2008

Bile on The Nervous Breakdown 2011

Small Talk in the San Diego Poetry Annual 2019-20

Elegy for Jim in The San Diego Poetry Annual 2020-21

Anti-Banana Poem in Beat Not Beat 2022

CPSIA information can be obtained
at www.ICGtesting.com
Printed in the USA
JSHW030936200822
29488JS00001B/3